# PROFOUNDLY SHALLOW

A COLLECTION OF UNCOMMON ESSAYS…

COMMONLY SO…

SEAN R.CABIBI

PUBLISHED BY GREY WOLF CAPITAL, LLC



This book was written by someone with just enough free time to avoid becoming productive, but not enough wisdom to stay quiet. Any resemblance to real events, people, or your last awkward family gathering is entirely intentional. If you find yourself offended, congratulations, you've read it correctly.

Cover design by The Downshift Frequency
Cover photo from the public domain via rawpixel, background image courtesy of keus1 via freepik under free license.

ISBN: 978-1-967544-04-2

For the bars and taverns… providing both the spirit and the spirits that flow through every one of these essays.

# TABLE OF CONTENTS


Profoundly Shallow — 1

Woke and Broke: The Pageant of Performative Progress — 4

The Tragedy of Gen Z's Money Woes — 14

All My Childhood Heroes Are Either Criminals or Degenerates — 22

If I'm the Best Man at Your Fourth Wedding, Am I Really the Best Man? — 25

Letting Cars Rot on Your Property: An American Tradition — 30

"I Can't Help It, I'm An Aries." No, Kate. You're Just a Bitch — 36

Heavy Demands: A Weigh-In On the Fat-Acceptance Movement — 41

Dave Chappelle: How Crossing the Line Could Mend Divisiveness — 50

Invisible Art: The Rich Using Real Money for Unreal Experiences — 56

You're Not Training to Work at Disneyland. You're Just a Furry — 61

Mainstream Acceptance of Crytocurrency Isn't Happening — 65

Is Using AI To Catch AI Also Cheating? — 70

I Know My Third-Party Won't Win, I Just Want To Fuck Over Your Candidate — 75

A Third-Party Voter Explains Why Kamala Harris Lost So Badly — 86

Hashtag Revolution: The Slacktivism of American Youth — 91

Redistribution 101: Leftist Students Meet Grade Equality — 97

Doomsday Cultists: The End of Days That Never Seems to End          104

Screaming Viking: The Origins of the Infamous *Cheers* Cocktail          109

You're Dedicated… But Are You Kamikaze Dedicated?          117

The 30-Minutes-or-it's-Free Pizza Delivery Guys From the 1980s
are the True Heroes          121

Smoke Detectors Can Save Your Life… I'd Rather Die          124

Your Will: Leave Enough So They're Grateful, But Not Enough
to Want to Kill You          131

Real-World Skills Should Be Taught in School, but Kids Still
Won't Give a Fuck          136

A Conversation with a Spirit is Not Credible Evidence          141

I Wrote About O.J. Simpson, but I Think it's Too Tasteless          145

On Second Thought, Fuck O.J. Simpson          149

O.J. Simpson's Legacy Will Be for a Record No Athlete Will
Ever Break: Double Murder in Minutes and Acquittal          151

The Weird Things You'll Find While Apartment Hunting          156

The Six Habits of the Highly Average, and How You Can
Be Highly Average Too          162

Famous Movie Quotes for Awkward Social Situations          168

I Can Tell What Kind of White Trash You Are By Your
Choice in Buffets          175

No One Cares About Your Social Media Politics… We Just Want
Cats or Titties   181

I Invited Two Jehovah's Witnesses Into My House   184

I Love You DoorDash, but We Need to Take a Step Back
On Our Relationship   189

My Rejection Letter from a Very Big Online Satire Publication   192

Think Globally and Act Locally in the Fight Against Climate
Change: Get a Pool   195

Kick a Gambling Habit by Betting $10,000 That You Can Do It   201

My Grief Counselor Was So Good, When He Died, I Didn't Care   207

How are My Chalk Outlines of Dead Folks Not Considered Art?   212

The Solution to America's Homeless Crisis: Move to a Better
Part of Town   217

Not Everyone Can Be A Doctor. The World Needs Garbage
Men Too… I Did Both   224

There Are Three Doors In Hell… And I Got To Pick One   228

Fakespeare: The Worst Writing Advice I Have Ever Heard   235

# Profoundly Shallow

Welcome, dear reader, to *Profoundly Shallow*, a book that dares to dive into the kiddie pool of modern life with the conviction of a philosopher and the floaties of someone who once read a tweet about Socrates. This collection of satirical essays is not here to change your life. Frankly, if your life is the kind that can be irrevocably altered by 2,000-word essays on something like the spiritual emptiness of online brunch culture, it was probably already teetering on the edge… and I respect that.

This book is for the thinkers who own books they've never read, for those who scroll, for the cynics who buy used textbooks that are already highlighted or double-tap their phones to deeply engage, and the philosophers who refuse to read beyond the headlines. Folks today are a tribe of sharp tongues and short attention spans, of deep feelings and shallow thoughts. Rather than fight it, we've chosen to celebrate it, preferably with a limited-edition oat milk latte in one hand and the vague sense that something is deeply wrong with everything in the other.

In *Profoundly Shallow*, I take a sharp, funny plunge into the chaotic ballet of being human… where beauty meets dysfunction, tapping ever so lightly into both the thought-provoking and deeply textured, as well as humanity's capacity to have the spiritual depth of scented candles. It's where the minutiae of daily life, social conventions, expectations, and annoyances permeate our souls as we maneuver through this spinning ball of dirt.

These essays will dissect modern absurdities with the precision of a gossipy scalpel. Expect think pieces on existential dread brought on by push notifications. Expect rants about the weaponization of anything and everything to justify… well… anything and everything. Expect a bold and probably unqualified look at humanity as a beautiful disaster that is full of sentiment while, at the same time, still being emotionally unavailable. Is it fair? No. Is it accurate? Well… kind of… sometimes. Is it funny? Hopefully.

However, beneath the irony, the sarcasm, and the occasional sentence written entirely in parentheses (like this one), lies a quiet reverence for the ridiculous. Because if you squint hard enough at the spectacle of modern life, if you lean in just close enough to the dumpster fire without catching your eyebrows on fire, you'll find something oddly beautiful. Something human. Something worth laughing at. Maybe even something worth thinking about… briefly… before your phone buzzes.

This book does not promise wisdom, but it may deliver clarity, if only in the sense that satire clarifies by distorting. Like a funhouse mirror held up to society, we'll travel around the warped, the exaggerated, the grotesque, and remind you that it was never really that different from the original image.

So, let's wade into the shallows. Splash around in the irony. Float on the surface of meaning. You may not emerge enlightened, but you'll definitely come out damp with insight… maybe. At least you'll be mildly entertained, and in this economy, that's practically enlightenment.

With that said, in the words of Captain Jean-Luc Picard: "One quarter impulse… engage."

I like *Star Trek*. Fuck off.

# Woke and Broke: The Pageant of Performative Progress

When Bud Light launched its campaign featuring famous trans influencer Dylan Mulvaney in 2023, they accomplished nothing positive for their brand… or anyone else, for that matter. They alienated their core market and didn't gain new customers who championed their progressive approach. What happened? Well, losing their core market was easy to figure out. A bunch of frat guys playing beer pong weren't identifying with a trans woman. They were clearly offended by the move. The more complex question is why Bud Light didn't attract new customers who were ready to support this new inclusive and progressive corporation and its products. There are two reasons for this. First, Mulvaney is largely seen by most, even by LGBTQ+ folks, as a grifter and opportunist who only transitioned because just being a gay man wasn't gaining her any fame or followers. Second, and most importantly, Anheuser-Busch (the parent company) is a global billion-dollar corporation. To the left, these huge corporations are the enemy, and one advertising campaign that rides a trend isn't going to change their minds about who they are.

Bud Light's failure is a glaring example of the shallowness saturating the woke movement. While this shallowness permeates everyone from corporations down to your average folks, it is most easily seen through the paper-thin actions of corporate America. Make no mistake… this is not just about corporate America, but we'll start here and work our way down.

First and foremost, let's be fair.

The truth is this: Not every corporation is comprised of evil, greedy folks sitting in boardrooms plotting the end of humanity for a profit. However, it is a fact that, historically, most corporations have shown little interest in anyone other than shareholders. I'm not criticizing them for this because that's their job… and I own a lot of stocks, so I'm not complaining. I'm only pointing out the fact that corporations' modus operandi is common knowledge, so when these companies go woke, it's not surprising that it lands like an amateur YouTuber trying to recreate a Jackass stunt. Yet, despite the obvious, corporations still pander to all kinds of groups to avoid any criticism, which inevitably only creates more criticism for their painfully transparent pandering.

Are you really surprised? This is Woke America. A world where you're measured not by your morals, your empathy, or your actions, but by how many buzzwords you can cram into a tweet without exceeding the character limit. Be it a corporation that runs commercials celebrating aspects of humanity that they never celebrated before (nor celebrate outside the time frame that we're all supposed to be celebrating), or influencers and celebrities, or regular folks that comb Google Images to find the right color square to make their new profile picture, the superficiality stands front and center. It's a beautiful land, rich in hashtags and ethical contradictions, where everyone is enlightened, inclusive, and ethically sourced… at least on social media.

This is a new world where justice is just a swipe away, activism is available on a subscription model, and folks really care about marginalized people… especially in months like June when they're celebrating Pride Month, or Earth Day in April, or February when it's Black History Month, or any other day or month that is recognizing and celebrating marginalized communities or other left-leaning issues. It really doesn't matter… we see the same messages repackaged for the specific group of people or issue being addressed. From corporations to the average Joe, America has always had a flair for performance, and the 2020s have offered the perfect stage for its latest production: "Wokeness: The Musical," starring a cast of billion-dollar brands, influencer-activists, and that guy you went to college with who now uses the word "intersectionality" in every sentence, even when ordering a sandwich.

But let's peel back the reusable bamboo curtain and take a good look at this brave new world because while the slogans are progressive, the actions are often depressingly retro.

For corporations, it's rainbows today, sweatshops tomorrow. For example, let's look at the month of June. It's Pride Month, which means it's time for every major corporation, from cereal brands to defense contractors, to roll out rainbow-colored logos, tweet something vaguely inclusive, and sell limited-edition Pride merchandise manufactured in factories where workers may or may not be allowed bathroom breaks. It's truly touching to see Lockheed Martin and Raytheon take a break from manufacturing missiles to remind us that love is love. Meanwhile, Nestlé will slap a rainbow on a chocolate bar and hope you don't notice the child labor allegations. Ah yes, nothing says "progress" like weaponized branding and conscience-cleansing capitalism. And it's not just Pride. Earth Day brings eco-friendly public relations campaigns from oil companies. Women's History Month features glowing tributes to female leadership from companies with a six-percent female executive ratio. What about Black History Month? That's when banks honor Black American voices by highlighting one intern and still charging overdraft fees in historically redlined neighborhoods.

Bottom line: It's all performative allyship that is all optics and zero substance. Think about it. Being "woke" has never been easier. You don't even have to care. All you need is the ability to copy and paste a paragraph into your Instagram story and say "I stand with [insert marginalized group here]." That's it. Activism, achieved.

Woke America is full of people who will loudly proclaim "Silence is violence!" right before they go silent when their favorite celebrity is caught doing something, you know, problematic. These same people will attend a protest, take a selfie for the 'gram, and then leave before things get too sweaty or the police show up. Then we have the misunderstanding that is inherent in short social media posts. Heaven forbid someone says the wrong thing, or you think they said the wrong thing… because in Woke America, intention matters less than optics. It's not about building bridges or educating. No, it's about public trials in 280 characters or less. You either vibe correctly, or you're canceled. It's like the Salem witch trials, but with better graphic design.

Along with corporations, we have to deal with the woke elite. While they're not big business, they are folks with a lot of money and influence who have a big impact when they disseminate their guilt… they just get to do it with a view. I'm talking about those spiritually awakened hedge fund managers and $80,000-a-year private school parents who speak fluent "woke" but live in gated communities on hills far above the madness with guard dogs named "Equity" and "Justice."

These are the folks who support defunding the police, unless someone's trying to break into their Tesla. They advocate for public education reform while ensuring their kids attend schools with tuition higher than most people's annual salaries. They post about food deserts while sipping kale smoothies imported from an organic mountain in Peru. To them, wokeness is less about systemic change and more of a lifestyle brand. It's something to display, like a limited-edition Banksy or a houseplant named "Robin DiAngelo." They'll quote James Baldwin at dinner parties, but still call the HOA on their neighbor for painting their mailbox a slightly disruptive shade of beige.

However, it's not just corporations or the rich elite. It's also everyday folks too. Maybe it looks slightly different from the fire escape of a modest apartment or the front porch of some basic suburban tract house, but the hypocrisy is the same, even if the motives are different. For middle America, going woke has all the same double standards, but the consequences for not falling in line can be devastating to those folks without deep pockets. At least corporations and the rich can afford to be canceled. Joe Six Pack's mouth can't write a check; his teeth can't cash.

To make matters even more complicated, the tide has shifted to include folks that are too woke. Yes, you now can not only get canceled for not being woke enough, but you can get canceled for being too woke.

The circus of cancel culture has evolved and is now dancing around the big top trying to make sense of itself. Initially, it was just a modern gladiator arena where public figures were attacked based on how viral their transgressions went. That eventually transferred down to anyone and everyone that behaved badly… but then it became anyone and everyone based on what others thought was an indiscretion, whether it was an indiscretion or not. It didn't matter what actually happened or what was said; it was what people "felt like it meant." That was the new truth. However, that pendulum swung when people started canceling those that were canceling others. Canceling someone over a perceived indiscretion was grounds to cancel those that were doing the canceling. It's gotten very complicated. Essentially, cancel culture is now the consequence for not being woke or, in some cases, being too woke.

Look at Bud Light and Anheuser-Busch. They were originally criticized for their marketing approach that focused on young white frat-boy types that cancel culture viewed as exhibiting toxic masculinity. Then they were attacked for being too woke with the disastrous Dylan Mulvaney campaign. Now, as of this writing, they have Post Malone, Shane Gillis, and Peyton Manning peddling their beer. Are they no longer woke? Who knows… we'll have to wait for the next trending issue to see if they are. My guess is they're still woke when it's fashionable to be woke during the specific time frame when they need to be woke, but only woke enough to not upset either side, if they even understand what that means. They might get canceled for being woke or not being woke enough.

They'll likely be canceled by somebody, for some reason.

In theory, cancel culture is about accountability, and it is still mostly used by the left for folks who are not woke. In practice, it often resembles mob justice with Wi-Fi. It's a spectacle: half Hunger Games, half high school talent show. Everyone gets a chance to moralize. Everyone is temporarily better than someone else. And then, just as quickly, we move on to the next digital villain of the week. Curiously, cancel culture tends to skip over, say, war criminals and billionaires hoarding wealth, and instead focuses on comedians who told a bad joke in 2012. Actual change? Too hard. But weaponized moral superiority? Now that's fun and engaging content.

Now, for the record, wokeness has actually created real change… at least for tech companies. Tech giants love wokeness so much, they've decided to program it. Algorithms now prioritize "inclusive" content, which sometimes means silencing other marginalized voices who get flagged for "aggression" when they dare speak truthfully. Oh, the irony. These same companies that ban controversial activists in the name of "safety" are also happily selling facial recognition software to police departments. And while they remove hate speech (sort of), they also allow misinformation to flourish like mold in a college dorm fridge. Meanwhile, social media posts about systemic oppression are written on smartphones assembled by underpaid workers in overseas factories with suicide nets outside. But hey, the new emoji update has a more diverse range of hand gestures, so… progress?

Real change also can be seen in universities, although when I say "change," I'm talking about how they operate and act… not actual real change. Universities are now temples of wokeness, places where every syllabus comes with three pages of trigger warnings and every seminar begins with a land acknowledgment read by a white professor wearing a Patagonia vest. It's a beautiful gesture, unless you ask what actual land reparations the school has made. Spoiler alert: it's zero. Meanwhile, tuition has increased approximately

974%, and adjunct professors teaching "Decolonizing the Canon" are paid in leftover hummus from the faculty lounge. Students are taught to interrogate privilege, but only after burying themselves in six-figure loans to access the education. Then, when a controversial speaker is invited to campus, the school either cancels them preemptively or hosts them anyway, but then barricades the building like they're preparing for the zombie apocalypse. Nothing says "academic freedom" like tear gas and a safe space flyer.

It's in the universities where folks also learn about the hierarchy of suffering. Enter the Oppression Olympics, where points are awarded based on how marginalized you are and deducted if you're ever caught enjoying a latte without critical commentary on colonialism. Here, the goal is not to build solidarity, but to out-woke everyone else. Intersectionality, once a powerful concept for analyzing interconnected oppression, is now a buzzword used to justify why someone should be given a platform to sell skincare. Instead of coalition-building, we get resume-style introductions like: "Hi, I'm a queer, non-binary, neurodivergent, left-handed vegan with Scorpio rising." And that's just the barista. It's not that identity doesn't matter… it does, deeply. However, when identity becomes performance, it loses its punch. Real activism is messy, slow, and often thankless… it's not viral, vibey, and full of aesthetic infographics.

So here we are… deeply aware, morally exhausted, and vaguely confused. Woke America has all the right vocabulary:

justice, equity, inclusivity… but somehow, things haven't really changed. The police still shoot. The ice caps still melt. Workers still starve, but hey, we got a new season of *Queer Eye*, so we're feeling better already.

Maybe the problem isn't wokeness, but how easily it's been co-opted by capitalism, by opportunists, and by institutions that would rather tweet about progress than actually implement it. Wokeness, in its truest form, is about awareness and action. But in America, we stopped at awareness and turned it into a lifestyle. What started as a movement became a market. What should've been a revolution became a rebrand… and in the process, we've created a culture that prizes appearance over action, performance over principle, and slogans over systems.

However, all hope is not lost. Beneath the noise, the hashtags, and the ethically sourced hoodies, there are still people doing the work. Quietly. Consistently. Without needing credit. They're not "going viral," but they're going the distance. Until then, we scroll, we post, we buy, we cancel, and we clap back, convincing ourselves that this, somehow, is justice.

Welcome to Woke America: Please recycle your virtue on the way out.

# The Tragedy of Gen Z's Money Woes

Once upon a time, not too long ago, young people were supposed to grow up, get an education, land a job, buy a house with a white picket fence, have 2.5 children, and spend their evenings enjoying casseroles and tax deductions. And we did that… although I'm Gen X, so I prefer pizza over casseroles.

Shortly after my generation aged into adulthood, things changed… and it didn't take long. Part of it is the gap between the rise in the cost of living and incomes that have remained relatively stagnant. However, the other part is the young folks who just complain about "how hard they have it" and "there aren't any jobs that pay enough to live." Today, we have a generation that can't afford guac at Chipotle without performing internal calculus on whether they can still afford rent this month.

Welcome to the chronically underfunded, emotionally overdrawn, and aesthetically curated lives of Gen Z, otherwise known as The Bankrupting Generation.

These young folks complain, and although I'm quick to clown on these kids too, let's take a step back and not be too hasty in our judgment. Complaining, after all, is a generational art form, finely honed and carefully selected with the same fervor as an Instagram grid. Maybe my generation, and previous ones, whined about walking ten miles in the snow uphill both ways, but at least we didn't have to choose between paying our electricity bill and subscribing to Netflix, which, let's be honest, is the only thing standing between them and an existential spiral.

The biggest gripe I hear is that no one can buy a home anymore. Basically, Gen Z constantly complains that the American Dream of homeownership is nothing more than an expensive mirage floating just beyond the reach of avocado toast-stained fingers. It used to be that you could buy a house for the cost of a modest used car and a firm handshake. Nowadays, unless you have a trust fund, a tech startup, or a side hustle selling NFTs of digital hamsters, homeownership is about as attainable as swimming with models and sharks at a FYRE Festival.

Young people today will tell you this with the hopeless tone of someone recounting a myth, like Atlantis or a functioning healthcare system. They say things like, "My parents bought their house at 23 for $80,000. I pay that in rent each year just to live in a closet with two roommates and a suspicious smell coming from the vent."

There is no doubt that real estate prices have skyrocketed while wages have politely declined to participate in the inflation party. This leads to the uniquely modern paradox of paying $2,000 a month in rent but being told by mortgage lenders that they can't "afford" a $1,400 monthly mortgage. It's like being denied entry to a party you've already been inside for five years, but suddenly your suit isn't fancy enough.

The irony in this house dilemma is they complain about not being able to own a house but voluntarily decide not to own anything else. For a generation where commitment seems to be feared on most levels, nothing says "eternal debt" like subscribing to everything from razors to ramen noodles. If life before was about accumulating assets, now it's about accumulating logins. They pay $9.99 a month for music, $12.99 for movies, $6.99 for meditation apps they open twice a year, $14.99 for Prime shipping on phone cases they didn't need, and $4.99 for a journaling app to write about how broke they are. But hey, you gotta spend money to feel like you're in control of your spending. Then, of course, there is rent, which essentially functions as a subscription to existence. Let's not forget student loans. These "subscriptions" have the deluxe plan. You can't cancel them... and the interest is auto-renewing, with customer service operated by AI that keeps telling you to repeat your account number ten times before it automatically hangs up on you.

The student loan debts are the absolute killer. Like herpes, they will follow you forever. In and of themselves, done properly, they can be beneficial... Gen Z still hasn't figured this out. It's been said that if you do what you love, you'll never work a day in your life. But what they forgot to mention is you also won't get health insurance. Many young people have taken this advice to heart and are now professional artists, freelance content strategists, or "creators," which is Gen Z slang for "unemployed, but my podcast is taking off."

Look, you can do what you love… but only if it pays well. If it doesn't, study in fields that actually have high-paying jobs on the other end. You might love philosophy, but last time I checked, they aren't building philosophy factories anywhere. Their parents, having spent decades chasing stability, encouraged their children to chase dreams, but that may have contributed to the problem. Sure, parents want you to chase your dreams, preferably ones that don't involve working at a Taco Bell with an MFA. Now, with student debt that rivals small nation-states and wages that barely beat inflation, many young adults have taken up full-time positions in their childhood bedrooms. The rent is free, the fridge is full, and the Wi-Fi? Excellent.

But let's not be too cynical. Living at home is now seen less as a failure and more as a "strategic financial regrouping." This is branding at its finest.

To be fair, it is true that everything has gotten very expensive, and that's a big part of the problem here. Why have things gotten more expensive? This is a reasonable question. I have no answers… shit sucks. I've seen eggs cost as much as gold-plated truffles, gas prices fluctuate with the drama of a teen soap opera, and even water now comes in boutique glass bottles with inspirational quotes. However, your generation isn't special. We all went through this. When I was in my 20s, I was so broke that even if I farted into my back pocket, it still wouldn't have a scent. When I got my identity stolen, my credit score went up 80 points. The difference is we got tired of making minimum wage and living with four guys in a two-bedroom apartment. We coped with it until we figured out a way to change the situation and executed a plan… it's a long game, but that's the game. Young folks? Nah… they have turned coping into culture. They make memes about not being able to afford groceries, laugh through tears as they Venmo each other $3 for pizza, and normalize financial trauma by calling it a "mood." It's like watching a generation collectively lose a game of Monopoly, but instead of figuring out a way to win, or at least flipping the board, they start a TikTok trend about it.

Now, I know there are millions of folks who will take my opinions and point to me as the problem. Generational blame... a favorite pastime of the financially tormented. While it's not entirely fair to blame older generations or this mythical benefit of growing up in "better times," it's hard to ignore that some of the cards seem to have been dealt rather unevenly. It may seem like previous generations enjoyed pensions, affordable education, job stability, and salaries that kept up with the cost of living, while today's young adults do not have those things. This isn't entirely true. Those things still exist today, but you're not likely to get them majoring in Rural Dance Theory or avoiding jobs that offer those things because they "don't spiritually align with your life's philosophy." Instead, young folks today get unpaid internships, gig work with no benefits, and a

LinkedIn feed full of people who are "humbled to announce" they got hired for a new job while you're humbled when you have to decide between a jar of peanut butter or jelly because you cannot buy both.

Then there is the Internet. You have it… we didn't. You can hunt for thousands of jobs and make contacts all over the country while eating cereal. Try riding 15 different buses a day traveling all over your mid-size town, filling out applications, and shaking hands in 105-degree heat wearing a shirt and tie. If we were lucky, those ten hours of living on public transit netted us ten job applications, half of which had already decided they won't hire you the minute they saw the long hair pulled back into a ponytail.

So, it's not entirely older generations' fault, and don't delude yourself into the fairy tale that we "don't understand the struggle." We do, just in different ways. Your job is to find out how to navigate this world, just like it was our job to navigate ours. The bottom line: Every generation has to figure it out. Look, there is no doubt the current economic system is a web of late-stage capitalism, deregulation, globalization, and probably a little bit of Mercury in retrograde, but that is too complex and multifaceted for young people to want to deal with… plus blaming Boomers is more fun and fits better on a tote bag.

Regardless of what I say, I do get that things are a challenge, and you could argue that these challenges are bigger than the ones we faced. It does seem like you need a full-time job, two freelance gigs, a weekend dog-walking business, and a TikTok channel just to afford two-day shipping on deodorant. Some have crumbled under this, others have moved in the total opposite direction and have turned "hustle culture" into a brand, complete with merchandise that says things like "Rise and Grind" or "Sleep Is for the Weak," even if the Louis Vuitton bags under your eyes suggest otherwise. Somehow, "working yourself to death" has been rebranded as "entrepreneurship." No worries. They're totally fine. They've optimized their calendars, color-coded their stress, and subscribed to three productivity apps that remind them how behind they are every morning.

This is another layer of irony with today's financially stressed youth: They're deeply skeptical of capitalism, yet wholly dependent on its infrastructure that not only provides them the technology that they would be crippled without, but the only route to change their current situation provides them the. They rail against Amazon, but still order with one click. They denounce billionaires, but find themselves retweeting them for clout. They fantasize about unplugging from the system and post on social media how much they want to disconnect from the system, and then provide updates… on how they have disconnected from the system. It's like the Internet version of being California sober.

In a way, it's not hypocrisy… it is survival. They know the game is rigged, just as we did 30 years ago, but opting out just means falling even harder. We knew it back then too. So they play the game, reluctantly, ironically, maybe even stylishly. What we need to understand is that the complaints of today's youth aren't just complaints… they're collective data points in a system that was never fair or kind, but now, in a world built on a nonstop barrage of information hitting them 24/7, most of it having little or no real value and just demanding every ounce of physical and mental energy. The memes, the sarcasm, the tears cried into tote bags… they're not signs of apathy, but signals of burnout. The key takeaway is this: This generation isn't lazy. They're resourceful, over-educated, underpaid, and incredibly good at pretending things are fine with the help of filters and phrases like "I'm thriving!" However, beneath it all, there's a very real plea for a future that isn't just a nostalgic relic of a past that no longer exists. We need to help them find it… but they also need to show that they want it; just like it always has been for every generation before them. It's fundamental that they understand that every other prior generation faced the same battles, just with different circumstances.

# All My Childhood Heroes Are Either Criminals Or Degenerates

The day they arrested Bill Cosby for drugging and sexually assaulting women over the last few decades was the final nail in my childhood coffin… the last pillar that held up my hall of heroes to officially collapse. It was heartbreaking and soul-crushing to come to the realization that, for Bill Cosby, the Sandra Bullock movie *While You Were Sleeping* was a biopic to him, not a romantic comedy. I looked up to this man my whole life. It was shocking, and I didn't want to believe it, but the allegations were pouring in from so many women, and it became clear that his behavior was well-known. It was an open secret in Hollywood.

Cosby denied it all, but he was hanging on by a thread. Seriously, at this point, what the fuck could Cosby possibly argue after all of this? That drugging a hooker isn't rape, it's really shoplifting? The eradication of my adolescence didn't start with Cosby's downfall, but it sure ended with him.

It's sad for children of the 1980s and 1990s. All of our heroes ended up being the biggest pieces of shit on the planet.

We're talking adultery, racism, steroids, accused pedophilia, and marrying your girlfriend's adopted daughter. That's just the start. Then you have double murder and kidnapping… a twofer for O.J. Simpson, who is still the GOAT of being a piece of shit.

When I was growing up, Woody Allen was revered for his writing and directing. He created some of the most iconic movies ever made. He was a genius then and still is a genius today… but he also married his long-time girlfriend's adopted daughter, Soon-Yi Previn. He dated her mother, Mia Farrow, for years, and they were a huge Hollywood power couple, and yet, somehow he ended up with Farrow's adopted daughter.

Allen is famous for once saying: "Eighty percent of success is showing up." Did he say that when he attended Soon-Yi's high school graduation?

Michael Jackson was considered a god during those decades and was the biggest star on the planet. Then he got into all kinds of trouble with accusations of touching children. He also got super fucking weird and turned himself into some kind of alien.

To be fair, he was never found guilty of any crimes, and I personally don't think he ever inappropriately touched kids, but let's get real. By the late 1990s, the dude was weird as fuck. He had so much plastic surgery and changed so many shades of color that, after his death, they could have melted him down and recycled him into a Rubik's Cube. Then it would be the children's chance to play with him.

Look, the point being that he's the best of the bunch… and that's not saying much.

Then there's Lance Armstrong: the motherfuckin' hero of heroes. He won seven Tour de Frances in a row after beating testicular cancer. This guy started a whole movement and likely willed cancer patients across the world, who otherwise would have died from giving up, to beat that disease. Then he tested positive for steroids and admitted that he was on them the whole time… a total fucking fraud.

Armstrong at least came clean and owned it. Never made any excuses, for the most part. I think he did say others were doing it, so he felt compelled to do the same. Nonetheless, I give him credit for admitting what he did. However, the irony of Armstrong coming clean about his transgressions, apologizing, and owning up to cheating was that he still didn't have the balls to do it.

Look, I get that everyone here is human, and I expect humans to make mistakes. But God damn, why does it have to be every one of my childhood heroes? Why were the mistakes these folks made not just small, forgivable transgressions? I'm living in a world where Hulk Hogan's adultery and racist rants still land him near the top of the "least worst" of my adolescent heroes.

Is that really a childhood anyone wants for their kid?

# If I'm the Best Man at Your Fourth Wedding, Am I Really the Best Man?

The announcement to our circle of friends and family seemed just as poignant and special as the other three times.

"Sean, I want you to be the best man at my wedding."

Everyone congratulated me with playful cheers and good-natured teasing. I should be honored, but I'm really not.

It's your fourth wedding. Am I really the best man?

Your first wedding you forgot to invite me. Folks had to remind you when they realized I was never put on the guest list. The second wedding, you at least remembered to invite me. The third, I was made a groomsman, but that was only after your cousin died in a car accident a few months before. I was a quick backup. A guy had to die in a horrific accident before I could get into that spot, and now you want me to be the best man for marriage number four?

Let's face it, you could have easily had all your friends play rock-paper-scissors to decide this, and it would not have made a difference. The honor would go to the guy that could win a game played mostly by first-graders. Don't get me wrong, I love my friend and I hope this marriage works out, but I just cannot get excited like this is something special, nor do I feel esteemed to be the best man on a wedding day that less than two percent of Americans ever experience.

That's no bullshit. Less than two percent of Americans reach four marriages in a lifetime. I guess, technically, I am special for being asked, but not in the traditional way you should feel special. Maybe I would feel different if I thought this was "the one," but after three tanked marriages, I've learned there isn't one… and there will most likely be more than four. Trust me, this isn't going to be his last wedding.

While my friend is a great guy, he's not long-term marriage material. The core problem is he isn't one to compromise, which dooms every marriage eventually, but he also has a knack for picking the most controlling women.

His first wife constantly tried to put his balls into her purse, and that wasn't going to work for him.

What does this mean?

For youngsters who have never been married, let me explain this in terms you can understand: Marriage is like deleting all the apps on your phone except one. That one app will be the alarm clock… and that alarm clock is totally controlled by your wife.

Now, I know this idea of the "controlling woman" is just a stereotype, but regardless, marriage is still about compromise… and men will compromise more than women. Don't believe that? Try hanging a painting of dogs playing poker on the wall in the living room and see how far you get with your wife. Then, after you're ridiculed for your choice in art, get equally as upset when she hangs her desired painting in its place. Let's see what happens.

And that's just a painting on the wall… nothing serious.

For my friend, he could never compromise on anything, and that just created a ton of resentment with his wife. It was a brutal back and forth that ended up with him never being able to do anything right in her eyes, so he eventually stopped trying.

His life became a philosophical conundrum: If a man is in a forest and there isn't a woman around, is he still wrong? His marriage to her was a lot like trying to read the Terms of Use on the internet. In the end, you just give up and go, "I agree."

So, the marriage went south because of their inability to compromise on anything, but the real anchor that sank that ship was their inability to compromise on how to spend money. She loved to spend it faster than he could make it. He told me that one night when his credit card was stolen from a bar, he didn't bother to report it because the thief was spending less than his wife.

Look, people make mistakes when they marry young. The problem is that the second can end up being a rebound relationship that will end the same way.

His second wife ran off with one of his best friends, Steve. She was nothing but problems from the beginning, and even he didn't really like her or trust her, but he married her anyway. That was a huge mistake, for obvious reasons, but that's what happens when you're lonely and desperate after a failed marriage. She was a total snake. This isn't my opinion alone. Everyone knew it, including my friend. When she ran off with Steve, my friend was devastated.

Not because she left, but because he really liked Steve. To this day, he still talks about how much he misses him.

His third wife was unbelievably hot, but also unbelievably self-absorbed and demanding. She had more interaction with social media than with any real person, including my friend. When she did interact with folks, it was always about her, and she let you know that in a condescending tone. It was like she was trying to be the most unlikable person on the planet. Mission accomplished.

Just to give you a taste of this woman's personality, these were her rules for the wedding:

1.) Please arrive no more than 90 min early.

2.) Do not wear any variation of white, even if you are sure it isn't white at all. This means no cream, ivory, off-white, etc. You will not be allowed in if you are wearing anything the bride deems as "too white."

3.) Women cannot wear their hair in any style other than a bob or ponytail.

4.) Women cannot wear any makeup except mascara. That is the only makeup allowed.

5.) Do not go onto social media after you arrive until instructed to do so.

6.) Use #(whatever it was) when posting anything about the wedding on any social media platform.

7.) Any photo posted of the bride and groom must be approved by the bride before it is uploaded to social media.

8.) Do not talk with the bride at all until instructed to do so, and you will only be allowed a maximum of five minutes of her attention.

9.) Everyone will toast with Dom Perignon Brut champagne. No exceptions.

10.) You must come with a gift valued at $100 or more to be admitted in.

Awww yes… this is truly love right here.

They say a man is incomplete until he gets married, which is true. After that, he is finished. You think I'm being hyperbolic? Consider this fact alone: There are only three situations in this country where a witness is required: crimes, accidents, and marriages.

Do I really need to elaborate?

Maybe I'm wrong or jaded… maybe it *is* an honor to be asked to take the best man role at a fourth wedding. Everyone else seems to think it's a big deal, and maybe they're right. What do I know? My wife tells me I never listen anyway, or she says something like that… who knows what she's yapping about.

Whatever.

# Letting Cars Rot on Your Property: An American Tradition

Recently, I bought a house with three acres of land on the outskirts of Contra Costa County in California as an investment. The house is nice and well-kept, and the property itself is well-maintained, for the most part. The old owner passed away recently, and his family wanted to get rid of the house.

This also included everything on the property.

I didn't just buy a house. I also bought 13 cars and trucks as well… a bunch of junk vehicles the old man had scattered about the three acres.

Don't get excited. None of these vehicles were classics or worth anything, but rather a mishmash of long-forgotten cars and trucks from the 1980s through the 1990s. One was a Yugo. Isn't that worth something? They made them for one year back in 1988, and they became the laughingstock of the automotive industry. It must be a "classic," at least in a loose sort of "cult-following" kind of way, right?

No. Even fully restored, it's worth less than the original sticker price. It was a piece of shit back then, and it has aged like boxed wine.

Why the fuck would you have a Yugo? Could this car even be restored? If you took it to a mechanic under the age of 35, he would probably think it's some old car built in Slovakia.

Be it a 1989 Honda Civic or a 1992 Mitsubishi Mighty Max, no car or truck on that property had any value or the potential for value. Even Fred Sanford would have called to have these hauled off years ago. What was this guy thinking? Well, to answer this question, I would have to ask the countless folks all over America what they're thinking as well. Sadly, having a fleet of rotting cars on your property isn't uncommon at all. Many Americans seem to have a gift for finding old cars that were just "too damned nice" to be thrown away.

It has to be one of the most American things I have ever witnessed: the desire to collect dozens of junk cars and let them rot on your property for decades. Next to baseball and the Super Bowl, this probably ranks near the top of America's great pastimes.

Now, a lot of people are going to tell me that these folks are planning on fixing them up one day, but I can't remember a time where I have actually seen that happen. They just sit. Maybe they think it complements the aesthetic appeal of their meth lab, or they cannot find enough space in their shed to store the cars because it's packed full of spare Ferris wheel parts collected from a failing carnival.

Look, I'm not trying to stereotype anyone here, but let's be real. I would put money down that most of these folks use the laundromat to double as a daycare center and take six-packs to funerals. If you still think I'm pigeonholing people that do this, think again.

It's not just rural America that has this problem. It's infested the suburbs too. One of the homes I own rests in a nice residential area… a typical tract-housing development. Three houses on the block have multiple cars just rotting on their property.

Directly across the street is a house that just had a new family move in. They brought with them seven vehicles: four that run and three that should be hauled to a junkyard. Parked on the street are three vehicles, all fairly new, and the family's daily drivers. In that driveway is a motorcycle that is also newer. However, that motorcycle is parked tightly between two wrecked cars. One is an old Honda Del Sol that sits on four flat tires, covered with a thick layer of dust, and doesn't look like it has been driven since it was built in the 1990s. The other is an old 1992 Pontiac Firebird that is rusting, dirty, and oxidized to the point where it's hard to determine if the original color was black or gray. Inside their garage, they have what looks like an Oldsmobile from the 1980s that is just as dilapidated as the other two cars in the driveway.

Four doors down, the folks there have two junked cars. One is a 1990s Chevrolet Camaro in their driveway, and the other is an old Mitsubishi Eclipse from the early 2000s, which is parked on the street. Both look like they could be used on the set of *The Walking*

*Dead.* They have two other newer running cars: one they park in the garage, and the other that usually sits on the street.

At the end of the block, there is a family that has three cars that run and two old pickup trucks that are collecting dust and cobwebs. The man who lives at that house seems to be attempting to fix one of those trucks, but that has been going on for over a year, and I still have never seen him drive it. Maybe he isn't fixing it. I don't know what he's doing to it. The truck sits in exactly the same spot it was when they first arrived in the neighborhood.

This really isn't anything new. This is an American tradition. When I was in high school, one of my best friends got a 1968 Chevrolet El Camino. It was definitely a fixer-upper, but it ran, and he did his best to keep it going. However, a few years later, the car was sitting in his parents' driveway dead. By this time, he had purchased a cheap, reliable used Toyota Camry and drove that for several years. He has had numerous other cars since. He kept the El Camino, telling me it's a classic and that he was going to fix it up eventually. Makes sense. It *is* a classic car.

Fast-forward nearly 30 years and nothing has changed. He has moved several times, got married twice, had kids, all of whom are grown up and out of the house. Last week when I came by for a barbecue, there it was, on the side of the house: the old, dusty, rusted-out El Camino.

I had to bring it up again.

"Why don't you sell that thing?"

"No way. I wouldn't get the value out of it versus if I sold it totally fixed up."

What value? I've looked up the car on several websites that sell these classic vehicles, and a 1968 El Camino fully restored sells for about $40,000. To be honest, this isn't bad. Assuming it took no more than $10,000 to fix up his car, he would make $30,000. However, taking into consideration what he paid for it back in 1995, which was $1,500, and the fees to re-register it, including the money he has put into it over the years in numerous failed attempts to get it running again, at what point is it simply not worth it? If he had taken that original $1,500 and invested it wisely in 1995, along with all the rest of the money he put into it over the years, he probably would have had a lot more of a return by now. He also wouldn't have had to deal with this old car that he has hauled around from house to house for the better part of three decades.

Now, admittedly, I'm not a car guy, as most of the folks that have these old, busted-up cars on their property claim to be. However, I'm going to call bullshit on that argument. One, if you were a car guy, you would actually be working on these cars. Two, most of the cars I see aren't classics, but worthless cars from the 1980s on up. These cars would cost more to fix than they would be worth after you fix them. Who the fuck wants a 1995 Honda Del Sol or a 1992 Pontiac Firebird? There is a reason they only made these cars for those few years, or discontinued classic cars like the Firebird in the 1990s. Unless it's a classic Firebird from the 1960s or

'70s, no one wants it. No one wants a Del Sol either. No one wanted one when they were first put on the market.

Now, I'm mostly Libertarian, so I don't really care if anyone decides to create a car graveyard on their land. In some cases, this violates city codes, and that's an issue they will likely deal with eventually. To each their own. Some people will say it does impact others, as it hurts the value of neighboring houses and properties, and I do agree with that. However, that's easily mitigated by folks calling city code enforcement and making these people deal with their "collection."

At the end of the day, I simply find this to be fascinating. Most people who collect something are usually adamant about the condition. No one collects beat-up sports cards, smashed-up coins, torn-up comic books, or really anything that is damaged or beyond repair. However, give some folks a collection of cars that look like they belong in the background of a post-apocalyptic movie, and it becomes the future restoration project they're going to start one day… and from what I have seen, that day is apparently February 31st.

# "I Can't Help It, I'm An Aries." No, Kate. You're Just a Bitch

I'm generally willing to believe in the possibility of just about anything, but astrology is one that has completely escaped me. Now, it's not that I don't believe in the possibility that astrology does have merit, at least in some small way; I'm just more baffled by how many folks fully buy into astrology. On top of that, these same people almost always use astrology to explain everything that happens to them and to explain their own behaviors.

The kicker is they do this without blinking an eye. They are fully convinced and committed.

Now, let's clarify. I'm talking about astrology, not astronomy. There is a difference here. One is a science; the other is a way for white women to place blame elsewhere for their problems, attitudes, and behaviors that won't get them called a "racist." Astrology is this idiotic belief that celestial bodies and their positions at the time of a person's birth can influence their personality, behavior, and future. This also includes the positions of celestial bodies over a lifetime as well. While it has been practiced for centuries, it wasn't until modern American white women appropriated it that it became both a way to be deeply spiritual and connected to higher existences, while simultaneously avoiding the trappings of traditional religion, allowing them to get drunk on Lemon Drops and blow random guys in bar bathrooms.

This is where we find ourselves at a crossroads. It's one thing to lean on this type of absurd foolishness to help guide you, but it's another to use it as an excuse for your behavior and your situation in life.

"I can't help it. I'm an Aries."

No, Kate… you're just a bitch.

Look, if you find your life has ended up being a mountain of regrets and disappointment, and you're acting like a total prick, it's not celestial alignments or planets. It's because you're surrounded by overdue bills you can barely cover, your man seems distant and stressed, your kids are overwhelming you, your job is beating your soul into the ground, and you own every middle-class luxury that should make you happy… but it doesn't, so you take it out on others. I'm not convinced you can start blaming planets for everything that's happening to you or around you.

However, if you still want to blame a planet for all of this, blame Earth. Welcome home. We're all dealing with the same shit you are. It's called life.

Two points of clarification before I continue.

First, if you think I'm coming off misogynistic because I keep saying "women," or you've noticed I'm specifically targeting women with this essay, I'm not. Trust me… I would love to include men in this critical examination, but dudes don't do any of this shit.

Tell me the story of one man that has ever come up to you and started discussing how Jarnsaxa has entered the third cycle with Saturn and its alignment with Hyperion is causing a negative fluctuation in three of his seven chakras.

You can't, because that has never happened... and if by some chance it has, that's not a man, not by any definition.

Two, I want to make it clear that I'm not being critical of those who use astrology to help guide them, but rather just those who use it as an excuse for their life situation or their behavior. You're free to be someone who couldn't pour water out of a boot with the instructions on the heel; just don't be a total dick and expect me to accept that Phobos is in retrograde and that's why you're acting like a douchebag.

Honestly, I do not care if people want to believe the position of the celestial bodies impacts their daily lives. In my opinion, Saturn aligning with Jupiter while Orion was in its second cycle is not the reason you lost your job... you're a drunk who drinks excessively all the time, so it wasn't some celestial occurrence that ended your employment. It was the handle of vodka you slam every day.

And I have real grounds to say this because the evidence supports it.

One of the most significant criticisms of astrology is its lack of scientific foundation. There is no scientific evidence to support the claims that celestial-body positions impact anything about you or your life. In contrast, astronomy, the scientific study of celestial objects, has repeatedly debunked astrological assertions. Astrology is just another way for folks to find a million excuses for whatever is happening to them or around them, and it is effective. Astrology is very susceptible to the Barnum Effect. This refers to the psychological phenomenon where individuals believe vague and general statements about their personality and life to be highly accurate. Astrology often relies on these vague and general descriptions of personality traits and situations, making it easy for individuals to interpret them as personally relevant.

For example, an astrologer might say: "You are outgoing, yet sometimes introverted," a statement that can apply to almost anyone. They also could say, "Your crushing debt, depression, and addiction to alcohol and low-grade amphetamines are because Caliban and Portia have crossed the center grade with Uranus, disrupting Proxima Centauri." Debt, depression, and the questionable use of substances? Nothing more American than that.

Astrology also is riddled with inconsistencies and contradictions. Different astrologers may provide conflicting interpretations of the same birth chart or celestial-body alignments, leaving individuals confused about their supposed astrological destiny. There are two possible reasons for this. One possibility is that it's a complicated science and reading astrological charts requires years of specific training. While some have achieved this level of superior astrological intellect and insight, that is no guarantee that all experts will read the charts in the same way. The other possibility is that astrology has the same scientific merit as a fart in a space suit and astrologers are just a bunch of charlatans preying on people who, if they were any dumber, would have to be watered twice a day.

Some might say that it is essential to approach discussions about astrology and the people who believe in it with respect and understanding. It is true that intelligence is a complex and multifaceted trait, and it could be perceived as unfair and unproductive to label individuals as "dumb" based solely on their belief in astrology. At the end of the day, we must realize that people from all walks of life, including those with different levels of intelligence, seek meaning, comfort, and guidance in various ways. Some will find these through astrology, while others will pursue different paths. Ultimately, understanding the appeal of astrology requires a nuanced perspective that acknowledges the complex interplay of cultural, psychological, and social factors in shaping individual beliefs and choices.

So, if you think I'm coming off as a complete asshole, I'm sorry. I can't help it. I'm a Leo.

# Heavy Demands: A Weigh-In On the Fat-Acceptance Movement

Once upon a time, society decided to stop shaming people for their appearance… and rightly so. After all, no one likes being judged for their body by strangers who can't even spell the word "thyroid," let alone understand what that even means. However, as quickly as society demonized folks for shaming people, the pendulum swung in the other direction, and that birthed the body positivity movement: a wholesome idea rooted in empathy, self-acceptance, and the revolutionary concept that humans come in different shapes and sizes.

On the surface, this isn't a bad idea, right?

Well… that wholesome idea is not quite what actually manifested. Instead of advocating for empathy, self-acceptance, and preaching the truth that humans come in all different shapes and sizes, things took a hard turn down an entirely different road. Somewhere along the ever-evolving enlightenment of our society, we went from "stop bullying people for being fat" to "cancel the doctor for suggesting exercise."

In the words of every exhausted American dealing with this: It escalated quickly.

Originally nestled comfortably between social justice hashtags and TikTok, the fat-acceptance movement started out as a call for compassion but quickly evolved into a full-blown ideology, complete with its own orthodoxy, contradictions, and a list of demands longer than a CVS receipt.

Let's all take a walk on the treadmill of logic and examine how a movement rooted in self-love has, at times, forgotten to pack common sense in its gym bag.

In the modern moral hierarchy, few groups enjoy more rhetorical immunity than the self-proclaimed "radical fat activists." Criticize a political party? That's a debate. Question inflation? That's discussing economics. Suggest that living on a steady diet of gravy and defiance might not be optimal? That's hate speech.

Yes, the fat-acceptance movement has elevated itself to an untouchable status usually reserved for endangered species and Area 51. Criticism is forbidden, nuance is fatphobia, and even well-meaning suggestions about health are a form of "body terrorism." Doctors who mention BMI? Oppressors. Nutritionists? Agents of the wellness-industrial complex. Scales? Shame devices created by Big Lettuce... and don't even think of saying the word "obese." That's a slur now. The preferred term is "person in a larger body," which is both more compassionate and infinitely harder to fit on a medical chart after you have a massive heart attack.

In recent years, the term "fatphobia" has become the catch-all label for everything from actual discrimination to basic facts about metabolism. It's not just a term for societal bias; it's a rhetorical bat swung at anyone who dares to suggest that maybe, just maybe, a triple-deep-fried lifestyle has its downsides. Language itself has buckled under the weight of this movement's definitions. What was once a plea for empathy becomes a demand for total linguistic obedience. You're no longer allowed to say "overweight." Say "larger-bodied." Don't say "struggles with health." Say "thriving in a non-normative body."

At this rate, even the word "fat" will eventually be replaced with "body-enhanced American."

This aggressive and intimidating approach is rooted, at its core, in the insistence that weight and health are completely unrelated. This is actually one of the movement's more entertaining contradictions. They'll claim that weight and health are completely unrelated… unless you begin questioning the movement, in which case they're absolutely related, and you're probably just jealous of how strong and empowered fat people are. Essentially, if a thin person posts about running a 5K, that's toxic fitness culture. However, if a plus-sized influencer posts a slow-mo video eating donuts in a bathtub? That's bravery.

To be clear, no one should be bullied for their size, but pretending that the laws of biology are just a thin conspiracy is… well, a bit of a stretch, even with elastic waistbands. We've reached a point where suggesting that weight might have something to do with diabetes or heart disease is greeted with the same horror as suggesting the foot-long hot dog you're inhaling is a sandwich. The data? Oppressive. The studies? Fatphobic. The lived experience of the cardiologist? Trauma-informed bias.

It's like watching someone fall down the stairs and then arguing that gravity is a social construct.

But aside from the ridiculous ideology, the group has a few things they want done. Yes, movements tend to come with demands. The civil rights movement asked for equal rights and access. The LGBTQ+ movement asked for equality and recognition. The fat-acceptance movement? It demands that airlines redesign seating, fashion brands re-engineer physics, and hospitals treat obesity with nothing but compliments and praise.

Let's be honest. There's a difference between asking society to be kinder and asking it to revolve around your caloric intake. For example, people started to complain that airplane seats are too small and then demanded the airlines build bigger seats or sell two seats for the price of one. When many of the airlines argued that would cost millions, the fat activists just stated that profiting off of pain is at the heart of fatphobia. If clothing brands didn't stock 6XL in every color, the fat activists said it was erasure. When retail managers replied that they only have so much inventory and the bulk of what is made is targeted to the "average," fat activists told them to think bigger… literally. If a health app asks for weight, that's a microaggression. When developers of these apps argue that asking is just part of keeping track of progress, the fat activists say that tracking progress is oppressive.

Perhaps the most mind-bending twist in the movement is its relationship with the concept of health itself. Depending on the day, fat activists seem to have different notions of what is actually "health." On Mondays, health is a tool of oppression. On Tuesdays, health is an individual's private business and no one else's concern. By Friday, it's a badge of honor… just not the kind that requires measurable indicators like blood pressure or cholesterol levels. We've entered an era where the phrase "health at every size" is taken literally. That's like saying you can hydrate with water regardless of the water's temperature, even if it's boiling. Yes, a person can technically be healthy at different sizes, but every size? Including the size where you can't walk up a single flight of stairs without reenacting the Hindenburg disaster?

However, to question this doctrine is to invite digital mobs wielding hashtags like torches, hunting you down in the middle of the village square. If a fitness instructor posts a video encouraging people to move more and drink water, the comment section would be screaming about being triggered and demanding that the post be deleted for espousing fatphobic garbage. Meanwhile, a self-described "fatfluencer" posts a "What I Eat In a Day" video featuring 8,000 calories and a two-liter bottle of ranch dressing with comments saying, "This is the representation we need." It's a world where recommending vegetables is problematic, but promoting sedentary lifestyles is "revolutionary." Where the real enemy isn't heart disease, it's the guy at the gym who dared to ask, "Hey, do you want a spot?"

Interestingly, while railing against thin privilege, the movement has developed its own elite class: the "acceptable" fat person. You know… the one who still has a symmetrical face, a jawline under flattering lighting, and just enough curves to be palatable on Instagram, but not enough to frighten airline companies. These are the chosen few who get brand deals, book TEDx talks, and say things like, "My body is political," while wearing $10,000 worth of jewelry.

For a movement so critical of capitalism, fat-acceptance activists have become shockingly good capitalists. The grift is strong, my friends.

There are now plus-sized lifestyle coaches, "anti-diet" dieticians, and "body liberation" consultants charging $299 for Zoom workshops on how to love yourself without changing anything. Merchandise abounds: T-shirts that say "Hot, Fat, and Unbothered." Coffee mugs that read "Calories Are a Myth." There are even online summits where the keynote speaker teaches you how to demand free gym memberships without the "going to the gym" part.

These aren't radical protests. These are Etsy storefronts with better branding. Suddenly, capitalism is fine as long as it funds a body-positive brunch series. Do you see the irony? Many of them are monetizing the very system they claim is broken.

A scroll through these fat activists' social media pages reveals a paradox: They shout "Down with diet culture!" while simultaneously promoting "gut health" teas and "body-positive shapewear." They mock "before-and-after" weight loss photos… until they lose 30 pounds and post one themselves with the caption: "This isn't for anyone else. This is my journey."

Personal accountability… suddenly it's in style when the algorithm smiles on it.

This movement has bled into every aspect of fitness culture, turning every health decision into a potential debate about the degree to which that decision attacks the "differently bodied person," or whatever term is en vogue this week. For example, going to the gym has now become a political act. Once the domain of muscle bros, soccer moms, and people who like to sweat near strangers, gyms are now battlegrounds in the war on body politics. In this new paradigm, if you post a photo of your gym progress, you're not showing personal growth or discipline; you're promoting a "thin-centric narrative" that could "trigger marginalized bodies." In this new world, fitness isn't about health; it's about aesthetics. If you pursue a healthy lifestyle, you might as well just issue a statement that you're not doing it to maintain health, feel better, or live longer… you're doing it just to "look good" and dismantle fatphobia. That's obviously what you're doing. There is no other valid reason, according to fat activists.

We've come to the point where, regardless of what you say and how you truly feel, the reason for your actions can only be defined by the fat activists… and this covers every area of the debate. It doesn't matter what evidence you have, the recorded history, the science, none of it matters because nothing supersedes the fat activists' "lived experience." This is the gold standard in modern discourse. A nutritionist may bring ten years of data. A medical journal may cite 200 peer-reviewed studies. But if a TikTok creator says, "I'm fat and I feel fine," science must now sit down and apologize.

Facts are fine, but lived experience is truth with seasoning.

This isn't to dismiss the value of personal stories. Lived experience brings texture to discussions. However, in recent years, it's been used as a shield against reality. If your "lived experience" includes being winded by tying your shoes, perhaps it's worth examining the idea of not celebrating that reality.

The movement also loves to weaponize outdated or misrepresented data. "BMI is a flawed metric!" they cry, which is true. However, they skip over the part where BMI being flawed doesn't mean morbid obesity is suddenly a healthy lifestyle.

The fat-acceptance movement, at its best, offers an important critique of the shame and cruelty historically directed at larger bodies. No one should be ridiculed for how they look. Compassion should never be conditional. But somewhere along the line, parts of the movement traded empowerment for entitlement. They've replaced shame with denial and accountability with applause. They've asked society not just to accept them, but to restructure itself to accommodate every demand, no matter how biologically or economically absurd. They say they want equality, but sometimes what they want is exemption: from facts, from consequences, from the laws of thermodynamics. There is a truth here, and the truth is this: Obesity is not a moral failing, but it's also not a moral virtue. Glorifying unhealthy lifestyles under the banner of inclusion doesn't liberate people… it leaves them stranded, cheering each other on in an echo chamber while quietly suffering the consequences.

We should love people of every size. We should treat them with respect and dignity, but we don't have to suspend reason to do so. Compassion is not incompatible with candor. At the end of the day, all movements should aim for the same thing: not just feeling better about ourselves, but actually being better… and no matter how you spin it, "body positivity" will never replace cardiovascular health.

# Dave Chappelle: How Crossing the Line Could Mend Divisiveness

Dave Chappelle is not just a comedian, but a modern-day philosopher. He quickly rose as an important voice in 21st-century social commentary. He's not the only one, either. Comedians like Joe Rogan, Bill Burr, Jon Stewart, Sarah Silverman… the list could go on for a long time.

And these folks may be our best hope to mend a deeply divided country.

Comedians deliver a unique blend with their social commentary and thoughts on our collective discourse. Not just because laughter helps bring us together, but because humor can also be utterly merciless, demanding everyone, regardless of opinions and attitudes, to authentically face themselves. It can hold an unrelenting mirror up to all of us.

Laughter is a universal language and the universal remedy that too many seem to have cast aside. In a world where every conversation seems to turn into a verbal rampage, it may be the only language left that we all speak… and that can also cool tempers. It appeals to everyone because everyone likes to laugh. However, humor can also be imposing and uncomfortable, and if done well, forces us to look at perspectives we would never see and truths we may find hard to swallow.

It's the unparalleled combination of these two things that may be the key to opening a real constructive dialogue, whether we want to talk about it or not.

Comedian Dave Chappelle is a good example of this.

Dave Chappelle's stand-up special *The Closer* erupted into a firestorm of controversy with his commentary about the LGBTQ+ community. Many on the left and in the LGBTQ+ community demanded he be cancelled immediately. Many on the right stood firmly on Chappelle's side, sick of woke culture they say attempts to destroy anyone who says anything that offends them.

Great comedians take no prisoners and compel everyone to put all their cards on the table. They have great power to drag us all into a dialogue using comedic devices such as satire, juxtaposition, irony, duplicity, and stereotypes to address taboo subjects that have polarized our nation. It's in this humor, even if it's uncomfortable humor, that they provide a unique landscape on divisive and complicated issues that no other form of "philosophy" or political debating could ever give us in today's world.

Chappelle did exactly this in *The Closer*. While his comments and jokes about the LGBTQ+ community are harsh and often vicious, littered with inappropriate language and stereotypes, it seems to be coming from a place of personal frustration.

In one bit, he discusses rapper DaBaby, who was cancelled by the woke left after he made homophobic comments during a concert in July 2021. But then Chappelle questions why DaBaby wasn't attacked by many of those same folks when the rapper shot and killed a Black man at a Walmart in 2018. His conclusion was that society cared more about some words that hurt the LGBTQ+ community's feelings than about the shooting death of a Black man.

"And this is exactly the disparity I wish to discuss," Chappelle clarifies.

He continues, saying folks are confusing the emotions he expressed.

"You think I hate gay people, and what you're really seeing is that I'm jealous. I'm not the only Black person that feels this way. We Blacks, we look at the gay community and we go, 'God damn it! Look how well that movement is going!' And we've been trapped in this predicament for hundreds of years. How the fuck are you making that kind of progress?"

As a Black man who has faced much of the same hate, and expressed those life experiences throughout his career with his own brutal racial critiques, his comments strong-arm us all into dealing with the same uncomfortable truth he has been dealing with his whole life.

Keep in mind, this is just one point he makes as he systematically breaks down these complicated ideas and the convoluted rhetoric on both sides. The intricacy of his thinking, the wit he possesses, his uncanny savviness, the multiple labyrinthine viewpoints, and the blistering truths he shares are poignant, emotional, and jarring… and yes, he often crosses the line. His comedy upsets many, infuriates others, and enrages groups small and large, but it also challenges us all, regardless of our principles, feelings, ideologies, and beliefs, to confront who we are. He questions humans' often irregular logic by putting our own hypocrisy on full display. It's a harsh reality, and no one is safe. This is not about jokes or offending people for laughs. It's about a larger discussion that needs to happen because we all need to hear it.

And you won't get this from the media.

Let's face facts: Media today is designed to separate, not educate. It's designed to mount forces, pick sides, and attack. I don't care if you watch FOX News or CNN; it doesn't matter. They have one agenda: my side is right, your side is wrong... and too many people want to live in this echo chamber that media creates. Social media is even worse with this contentious and discordant approach.

Comedians, on the other hand, are ruthlessly aggressive and uncompromising, calling everyone out on their bullshit, and doing so with intellectual acuity and humor... something that is painfully nonexistent in both media and social media.

This approach may be the only key to breaking down the walls that divide us. For the most noted and famous comedians, the mastery of their craft may be our best chance to start a real conversation about who we are as a society.

Comedian Sarah Silverman shares just how powerful humor can be in her 2017 stand-up special *A Speck of Dust*. In one bit, she talks about being at a protest in Texas where a young woman was holding up a sign reading "Abortion is Bloody Murder." Silverman, who leans left and is pro-choice, said she approached the woman with an empathetic frame of mind, realizing that the young woman and she were the same person, despite their politics being on opposite sides. Just like her, this person was a product of their upbringing.

"I'm a product of how I was raised, and these people were raised by people who loved them, who said, 'There are people out there that want to murder babies!' And if I was that kid, I'd be like, 'We have to stop them!'"

She continues, saying the encounter got heated. The young woman lashed out at her.

"'God hates you!' And I was like, 'Do you really think God hates?' And she goes, 'Yeah, he hates you!' And then I told her a doody joke."

At this point, Silverman pauses for a second, and then impersonates the young woman's reaction, who was trying not to laugh.

"It really is the great unifier."

Too many people are afraid to cross a line and only want to be on what they see as the right side of history, but comedians don't see it this way. The only way to be on the right side of history is to cross the line and force everyone to go with you… all of us, equally uncomfortable, and do this through a mixture of unique and humorous perspectives. It may be the only way to compel a conversation this country badly needs. Your politicians, your news outlets, your activists, your pundits, partisan hacks, and social media mobs do not want that and, frankly, do not possess the savviness, cleverness, or astuteness when it comes to context, nor the unpleasant grace that comes with delivering a stinging bit flawlessly with unyielding poise. How can we ever authentically deal with the line that should never be crossed unless we cross it?

# Invisible Art: The Rich Using Real Money for Unreal Experiences

When the hype surrounding NFTs first hit the mainstream radar, many folks mocked the idea of paying outrageous amounts of money for these digital items and crypto collectibles. In March 2021, an artist named Mike Winkelmann sold a piece of digital art for $69 million. While many of us scratched our heads at such a questionable purchase, at the time, we all believed it was possible these NFTs might be the real deal. At least we know the buyer did get *something*.

How about paying $18,000 for nothing? That actually happened.

In June of 2021, a buyer at an auction in Italy purchased an invisible piece of art... an immaterial sculpture, to be exact. The piece, titled *Io Sono*, is... well... a sculpture that isn't there. It's invisible. Despite what the artist claims is there, those of us with two eyes and no history of sniffing glue saw nothing.

I have no doubt the person who bought the sculpture was moved by it and genuinely thinks it's an astonishing and unreal piece of art. Most everyone else thinks it's unreal too... just not in the same way. Did this happen because people have too much money, or do they believe this has some actual value? For most of us, we probably see this as a byproduct of too much money. There are only so many houses, cars, boats, planes, expensive jewelry, or other luxury items one can buy. At some point, you find yourself looking for any reason to spend because you have so much money sitting around. If this was the case, then I can't knock someone for doing it. You can spend your money any way you want, even if it's on nothing.

However, in the case of the invisible sculpture, the creator attempted to explain what he was selling and what the buyer was actually buying… and the buyer seems to be on the same page. In a move that would rival Belle Gibson's explanations for her cancer, the artist, Salvatore Garau, claimed there is something there, even if we cannot see it. Using the theory of the Heisenberg uncertainty principle, Garau said that nothing still has weight; therefore, the sculpture has energy that is condensed and transformed into particles.

What?

It's one thing to sell empty real estate; it's another to attempt to legitimize it and then tell those of us who still live on planet Earth that we're too narrow-minded or uncultured to "get it."

I don't "get it," but more importantly, I can't "see it."

This isn't the first time something like this has happened, and it certainly won't be the last.

In the early days of the App Store, an app was launched called *I Am Rich*. The app cost $1,000 and was described as a "work of art with no other function at all." Essentially, it just showed folks that you're rich because you could waste $1,000 on a useless, non-functioning app. While Apple did remove the app after about a dozen downloads, similar apps popped up shortly after, priced between $200 to $500… and people bought them.

What is going on here?

I have a theory as to why this type of thing happens. It's not about having too much money nor stupidity. It's about a unique experience and a story to tell, something I believe wealthy folks value. And for them, it may not matter if it's genuine because they can just convince themselves otherwise.

Let me explain.

There is a documentary that came out in 2016 called *Sour Grapes*. It's about a guy who has an exceptional palate for wine and uses it to defraud rich folks in the vintage and rare wine market. Essentially, he would mix cheaper wines together to recreate the flavor of these rare and expensive wines, counterfeit bottles and labels, and then sell them at auctions.

In the documentary, they interview a man who displays several bottles of counterfeit wine he had bought over the years as an example of just how rampant fraud is in the rare and expensive wine-collecting world. He said that wine collectors and connoisseurs are a perfect target for frauds because the folks into collecting and drinking these wines really want to believe they have this extremely rare or vintage bottle and value the adventure of sharing those stories and experiences with others more than the money they lost.

It's not only about bragging, but something beyond that. They can share something that is very rare or exclusive with friends and acquaintances. They also now have a story to tell the world, with others who will corroborate the story.

"I once had a Romanée-Conti 1945 at the home of Maximilian Money Powerson, and let me tell you, blah, blah, blah. Jolene was there too. Remember?" And then Jolene would chime in with her recounting of events as well, like some big rich echo chamber of elitist social masturbation.

The man being interviewed said these folks convince themselves it's real, even when they know it's fake, because the experience and the story are much more important to them.

Maybe that's what we're seeing here with this immaterial sculpture. Some rich guy has it displayed in his house, and every time someone comes over, he'll ask the guest if they have ever heard of the immaterial sculpture *Io Sono*. The guest would recognize the unique piece from the publicity, and the host would then escort him to the art wing of his mansion so they can both stare at nothing in amazement.

In reality, they both know it's all nonsense but will convince themselves otherwise. That experience will carry on to the next gathering. The guest would eventually be with another group of rich folks, and he would let them know what he experienced: "I was just at the house of so-and-so, and he has the *Io Sono* immaterial sculpture." Everyone would let out a sigh of astonishment, and the person would continue, regaling his audience with the incredible experience of seeing the sculpture in person… even if he saw nothing.

However, at the end of the day, they all know deep down it's rubbish, but that's not what's important to them. It's the experience… whether they were drinking real rare wine or something counterfeit, or whether they were looking at a real piece of amazing art or staring into space.

I get that the artist and buyer would disagree with me. They still would claim there is energy there and it's real. I buy energy every month through the local utility, and I can actually show it to you, unlike *Io Sono*. Let me turn on a light. See that? If you're interested, I can sell you the bulb for $50,000. Sadly, there is probably someone out there who would buy that bulb for $50,000 if I pitched it as some unique or distinctive piece of art. The buyer would travel through elite circles of high society and tell the tale of how they bought my art piece *La Lampadina di Cabibi*. He would then invite everyone to come by for a fine dinner, drink expensive rare wine, or maybe fake wine… it doesn't matter, and stare at a light bulb they bought for the price of at least two more immaterial sculptures.

Maybe that's a sign of too much money… maybe it's just the price of an experience and a story, even if they all know the experience and the story are built on a mountain of bullshit.

# You're Not Training to Work at Disneyland. You're Just a Furry

Growing up in Los Angeles, it isn't hard to find yourself in the entertainment industry. Even though I was not really interested in acting, I still landed a McDonald's commercial when I was nine years old because my father worked in Hollywood. Many of my friends not only found themselves with similar opportunities, but they actively pursued gigs in entertainment as adults.

One of them, Stevie, was obsessed with Disney, and he dedicated his life to becoming a character actor at a Disney-themed park.

This isn't an easy gig to get.

It's a grueling audition process that requires acting skills, dancing, and the right look for many parts. Even if you make it through, they are constantly evaluating changes in your physical appearance, and they can let you go at any time if they feel you are unable to play a character.

Height, weight, and ethnicity are vital and must be specific because there are duplicate characters out in the parks performing at any given time. If Snow White is perceived to be a 5'7", 115 lb. white woman, then all women playing that character must fit that description. If a kid sees Snow White and then, 30 minutes later, sees her again but she's grown six inches, put on a few pounds, and is now Black, it ruins the illusion. You also can't be Cinderella at 35 or Peter Pan if you have a five-o'clock shadow and a receding hairline.

Obviously, those in full costume don't have this issue necessarily, but that doesn't help them during the initial audition, where the more characters they can play increases their chances of getting hired.

Despite all of this, it was my friend Stevie's dream. He had to train hard… and he did.

With a full Chip 'n' Dale costume, Stevie began traveling to conventions with others interested in this type of career. From Los Angeles, to Las Vegas, to New York, to Boston, to Orlando, and so on. This dude was going to these character conventions almost every week. According to him, it was a few days of intense training, such as role-play to get various characters down, learning how to navigate these bulky full-costume suits, and how to best express emotions and thoughts through movements since the characters did not talk.

Sounds legit… or as legit as this type of shit will ever sound.

However, then the stories got a bit blue as he talked about the partying they would do after training. It was typical stuff, like hitting the bars and clubs, drinking and dancing, and the like. Doesn't seem like anything that odd… until he said they go out still dressed in full costume and acting in character. This included the wild after-hours alcohol- and drug-fueled sex that followed… again, still in full costume.

Dude, you're not training to be a Disneyland character… you're just a furry.

One convention after another, for years, and this dude still couldn't land a gig at Disneyland or Disney World. Eventually, he just started working at various carnivals, circuses, and other traveling shows portraying generic or knock-off characters.

The pay was marginal and the advancement opportunities were nonexistent, yet he continued with the narrative that this was all about becoming a Disney character. However, most of the stories he told about his job centered on the freaks that worked these traveling shows and the sex parties they had.

You're dressed as Tigger, fucking a cartoon canine. This isn't training for Disney, unless slamming Pluto from behind doggy-style is your idea of studying. You may learn something about the term irony, but it won't help you understand the character better. What did you discover? Pluto likes it ruff?

Additionally, fondling yourself while Goofy goes down on Scooby-Doo will give you good insight into just how quick your entertainment career can spiral down and how brutal Hollywood can be, but it won't give you any new knowledge about character motivations, acting, or how to land a role at Disney World. What you do learn is that the entertainment industry is a dog-eat-dog world. Unfortunately, your specific understanding of dog-eat-dog doesn't make you a veteran of the Hollywood grind, just a warped voyeur.

A few months ago, Stevie worked this strange avant-garde rodeo that didn't have real animals, just folks dressed as the animals interacting with the human cowboys. At the end of the show, one of the cowboys was blowing some dude dressed as a steer… and that was just the start of the after-rodeo festivities Stevie told me about. He tried to convince me that it's not about the parties and that he learned a lot about acting techniques when animals must stay in character around humans.

Seriously? You expect me to buy that? It was a bigger load of bull than what the cowboy swallowed.

Look, if you're into this, that's fine. I don't judge. Live your best life. Just do us all a favor and quit with the "I'm an actor" façade. You're a furry.

Now, personally, I couldn't get into this type of shit, but admittedly, when he told me this one story about a dude dressed as a chicken fucking a girl dressed as an egg, I was intrigued. For that, I would have stayed to watch until they were done. Not because I'm turned on by this particular arrangement, but I would have to know the answer to one of the biggest mysteries that has plagued mankind for centuries. Wouldn't you want to know?

# Mainstream Acceptance of Cryptocurrency Isn't Happening

Several weeks ago, I was at a friend's house who was losing his mind at the same rate that Bitcoin was losing its value. It seems a string of unfortunate events in the market was kicking the living shit out of cryptocurrency. I guess my ignorance of how make-believe virtual coins work saved me a lot of money… you see, I invested in those ancient old-man things, like stocks and real estate.

This whole cryptocurrency revolution probably isn't as dire as I make it out to be, and it's even recovering as we speak, but I don't think this is going to ever be a mainstream currency used by the vast majority of folks. The argument that I'm wrong is generally made by hipsters or elitists trying to look edgy, smart, savvy, and cool… or a bunch of angry loudmouth so-called experts that seem personally offended that I would ever criticize their imaginary Internet money.

I know what you're going to say: blockchain, NFT, Metaverse, stablecoin, or whatever new verbiage gets your virtual panties wet. I'm not dumb. I know what all of these basically are, but I also know the basics of insurance statistics too. Doesn't mean I care to know more… and no matter how much you insult me about my ignorance and stupidity, I'm still not going to trade in my numerous California rental properties and dividend stocks for a large stake in Dick Twist Coin, Rocket Moon Can't Fail Coin, or a Bored Ape… or whatever project that's guaranteed to be the next revolution after the collapse of the last thing that was guaranteed to be the next revolution.

Despite cryptocurrency taking a bath recently, it will likely recover, all joking aside. Hell, I own some Cardano, and I'm holding it for the long play. I don't know much about Cardano or what the fuck it actually does, but everybody that claims to know anything about crypto just got their asses dragged across the rocks, so does my ignorance of Cardano really matter at this point? I guess we're all still learning… whatever the fuck that means.

Outside of that, I have realized that cryptocurrency will likely never be a mainstream accepted currency. One of the biggest problems is its volatility and how quickly it can shift, which hurts its viability as a form of currency that could be used daily. Take Bitcoin as the main example. This is, by far, the most legitimate and stable cryptocurrency in existence, and it fluctuates constantly. Sometimes a lot, sometimes just a little, but regardless, it moves. Fiat currency does too, but fiat shifting is not even close to the margins of Bitcoin, or any other cryptocurrency for that matter.

Imagine buying a pizza using Bitcoin and then, years later, realizing you spent $213 million for it. And that's in a down market… Pizza ain't that good. This will always make using cryptocurrency like regular money undesirable to the buyer as well as to the seller. Crypto operates more like a volatile stock, and unless it can stabilize, most folks will never see it as a currency.

Another major issue is the fact that most mainstream folks really have no clue what it is, how to get cryptocurrency, where it is, how it works, how to use it, or how to store it, and simply do not trust it… and they don't care to figure all of this out. Fiat currency to them is easy to understand, it's tangible, familiar, safe, accepted everywhere, and backed by government. To the mainstream, fiat currency works perfectly. Why would anyone want to switch to a more complicated system? We're Americans. We bitch when we have an entertainment system with more than two remotes.

The fact that cryptocurrencies can just be created out of thin air is another major problem for mainstream acceptance. It seems like anyone can do it… and it seems like everyone does. Most of these projects, like 99% of them, are clearly scams, pump-and-dumps, and jokes. For the few projects that are legitimate and trying to establish themselves as credible, this never-ending flood of scams will forever hold legitimate projects back.

When you try to tell me I'm just a moron and I don't know what the fuck I'm talking about, you're probably right. I really don't know. However, you'll be doing that with stories about Safemoon, Celsius, and HawkTua, as our backdrop while you verbally destroy me. Unless they can stop the creation of new scams, eliminate the fraudulent ones that exist, and create an industry where 99% of new projects are legitimate, cryptocurrency will remain beholden to the company it keeps. When most of those companies create questionable cryptocurrencies, fraudulent projects, joke coins, and scams, that's who you are as well in the eyes of the mainstream.

The current reputation of Bitcoin also poses a serious hurdle for cryptocurrency to enter the mainstream. It has been around for more than 15 years. It's by far the most legitimate, credible, and trustworthy cryptocurrency... yet only a small percentage of businesses in America accept Bitcoin. In 2025, approximately 2,300 businesses take Bitcoin. In America, there are over 32 million businesses. The most trusted, longest-existing, and valuable cryptocurrency, after more than 15 years, is still only accepted by 0.0071875% of American businesses.

The fact that only a few businesses take cryptocurrency is just one major issue. Another problem digital money faces is the ways it is accepted, and it's the one most mainstream Americans associate with this currency: it's used for questionable dealings. Mainstream America still sees Bitcoin, and cryptocurrency in general, as "the money criminals use to do bad things." Oddly enough, this really isn't even true, but the fact that scams keep popping up every day with cryptocurrency just adds to the idea that cryptocurrency is primarily money either used for illicit activities, or the cryptocurrency itself is the illicit activity.

Outside of these practical reasons, there is one problem that dooms cryptocurrency on a larger scale, one that would launch it into a huge political firestorm. If Bitcoin, or another cryptocurrency, did become a standard form of currency and a true competitor to fiat currency, it becomes a problematic social issue. Many folks in struggling communities across America who are already underserved, underbanked, or have no bank account at all, cannot get credit cards or debit cards, and live in a day-to-day cash world, could be excluded from this form of currency. Even if they had access, or just some access, many may struggle or fail to even understand how cryptocurrency works, since even the basic understanding of what it is, where it is, how it works, its value, and how to store or access it, requires both technology and some medium-level understanding and trust that often is scarce in many underserved communities. Cryptocurrency, if it became mainstream, may ultimately be viewed as a racist or classist currency that alienates those in most need… a way to deny many access to the main way we survive: Money.

Even if cryptocurrency can weather every other storm, it will never be accepted if, in fact, it created a world where those that "get it" get the money, and those that don't, oh well… guess they'll need to read up on blockchain, ledgers, and virtual wallets. It's complex and utterly moronic at the same time. Between the complicated world of cryptocurrency and the stupidity of people paying $2.25 million for a digital picture of a monkey, it's a fine line between intellectually groundbreaking and eating Tide Pods. Either way, mainstream America is not trading in their fiat currency to get into this fuck mix.

# Is Using AI To Catch AI Also Cheating?

You still write by using your brain? Why don't you just get a quill and a large scroll to draft your new book on? Fuck it… just get a chisel and carve your newest essay into a cave wall. Quit living in the past. Artificial intelligence is the future, and the future is now.

I get it, though. Let's get serious. No one really wants to read AI-generated writing, and for school purposes, it's considered outright cheating. For those who still actually write, using AI-generated material becomes extremely personal to them, especially when other "writers" produce AI-generated content and then enter this community acting like they're an "author." Nothing infuriates writers more than someone who openly uses AI, acts like they're a writer, then gets upset when you call them out on it, often looking at you arrogantly, like you're the one doing it wrong because you're actually writing.

"Okay, Boomer… whatever."

The question then becomes this: How do we filter out what is AI-generated and what is human? The answer? Use AI.

Not only can AI write your book, your articles, your term papers, create art, and help you avoid cooking dinner by generating grocery lists that always conveniently "forget" the ingredients, but now AI is also here to catch other AI doing these things. Welcome to the AI Ouroboros… an endless loop of robots policing robots, while the rest of us watch with popcorn and a solid amount of mild panic.

But wait, let's back up for a moment. AI detecting AI? Aren't you the ones bitching about people using AI in the first place? You say it's cheating… be it actual cheating in school or some form of "shortcut" that, at best, is deceptive or even unethical. Is that correct? If that is how you feel, then how can you justify using AI to detect AI? Isn't that also considered cheating?

Buckle up, because this rabbit hole is about to get more complicated than trying to explain blockchain to your grandmother.

So here's how it goes: You've just handed in your beautifully written essay to your professor. It's eloquent, sharp, insightful… and definitely not entirely your own work because, well, you may have gotten a little help from intelligence of the artificial persuasion. No big deal, right? After all, you used the AI ethically. It was just for a nudge in the right direction. It's like hiring a tutor, but the tutor happens to be a robot that works for free and doesn't judge your life choices.

But then your professor runs the paper through AI-detection software, and guess what? That AI figured out that another AI helped you. Suddenly, you're caught in the AI-powered spotlight like a raccoon in a trash can, guilty of not just plagiarism but, apparently, robo-plagiarism by the same technology that they're trying to catch you using. The humans have been bypassed altogether here.

So now the question looms large: If AI can be used to detect AI, is the real crime using AI… or getting caught by AI? Suddenly, AI is both your accomplice and your snitch… that backstabbing bitch.

Here's where we start the downward spiral of AI. Let's say you start thinking ahead and figure, "Hey, I'll beat them at their own game." So, you decide to use AI to check if the AI-generated content you just wrote will be detected by another AI. You're running AI to check for AI's AI-ness. This is like hiring a detective to follow a detective who's following you.

Of course, in this dance of digital detection, you've essentially created a paradox. The more you use AI to disguise AI-generated content, the better the AI detectors get at sniffing out AI-generated content. It's a cat-and-mouse game, but with less fur and more binary code. You end up stuck in a loop where each iteration of AI improvement is met with another AI countermeasure, until, eventually, everyone's too confused to care whether a human was involved at all.

And really, who's the victim here? You, for trusting AI to cover its own tracks? The professor, now wading through 17 different layers of AI-detection reports? Or the AI itself, forced into this ethical quagmire of self-betrayal?

Let's get philosophical for a moment. If you use AI to detect AI, are you also cheating the system? Isn't this like taking a calculator into a math test where the only goal is to find out if calculators were used? Sure, you're following the rules, but doesn't it feel like you've tricked everyone, including yourself?

What if you didn't use AI, but you run your work through AI-detection software just to prove you didn't? Do you get extra points for being proactive, or does this just raise suspicion? It's like trying to prove you're not a vampire by standing in front of a mirror. The fact that you even considered it makes everyone a little uneasy.

And if we go even deeper, is the AI itself cheating by doing our dirty work? After all, it's learning from our language, our habits, and our inability to write a decent conclusion paragraph. Who's really being taken advantage of here? The line between user and tool is blurring faster than my understanding of tax law.

Now imagine this escalating to its natural conclusion. At some point, we'll have AI detecting AI that detects AI detecting AI, spiraling into an infinite loop of machines hunting machines, while humans become mere spectators in a dystopian version of a professional wrestling match. There will be no winners... only AIs endlessly canceling each other out like some hyper-advanced, algorithmic version of rock-paper-scissors.

Eventually, the only way out will be for us humans to throw up our hands and say, "You know what? Maybe we should get involved again." And just like that, we'll find ourselves writing our own essays and drawing our own pictures, having come full circle. However, I doubt that will happen. As AI gets more sophisticated, we'll likely all stop caring about who or what wrote the essay, drew the art, made the music, and produced the video. Maybe we'll embrace the AI-generated chaos and just let the machines hash it out amongst themselves while we sip coffee and quietly reflect on our own obsolescence. After all, if everyone is using AI, is anyone cheating anymore?

Just like this article you're reading… is this AI-generated? If you think so, you're probably not happy that it exists and has my name attached to it as the author. I didn't write it, so you suspect, and that is an insult to all the real authors out there who put their heart, soul, passion, and time into their work for someone like me to simply generate an entire piece in seconds and put my name on it.

However, there is only one way to find out… use AI to catch me. You cannot be certain these days what is real and what isn't. The only certainty is that somewhere, somehow, an algorithm is watching… and it's probably better at judging you than your mom.

# I Know My Third-Party Won't Win, I Just Want To Fuck Over Your Candidate

When I stepped into that voting booth on November 5, 2024, I punched the ticket for Libertarian candidate Chase Oliver. For the record, I am a registered Libertarian and generally agree with most of the party's ideology, but even I have to admit that many folks who identify as Libertarians are fucking crazy. However, I didn't just vote for Oliver because I align with his platform… and I'm not delusional. I knew the outcome was going to be a loss from the beginning, but there was more to my vote than what many may think.

I didn't expect my nominee to win this election; I just wanted to fuck over *your* candidate.

And I didn't care which one. Donald Trump, Kamala Harris, or Joe Biden, if he stayed and hadn't been forcefully removed halfway through his campaign, it didn't matter to me. They were not just terrible candidates across the board, but three of the *worst* ever presented to the American people. To make matters even worse, it wasn't the first time two of these three clowns were thrown at us. That's probably the worst part of the election process over the last few cycles. It's like the two major parties actively search for even worse candidates than the last ones, and when they cannot find candidates that are worse, they just give us the same two candidates again. You don't believe this is what they're doing? Remember George W. Bush and everyone saying, "It can't get any worse than this."

Guess what? It did… way worse.

Let's take a look at the tape.

We'll start with Donald Trump, the thin-skinned, insensitive, childish, moronic fraud of a business guru whose campaigns and presidency were, and still are, nothing more than glittering generalities delivered as real solutions to actual problems… all wrapped up in nonstop self-congratulatory grandstanding and the continual narcissistic self-celebrations he called "rallies."

His failures are numerous, such as how he didn't effectively manage the COVID-19 pandemic, both in terms of public health response and communication. Now, I'm not here to vocalize my feelings about the coronavirus. That's not the point I want to make about Trump's response. Whether or not you think the coronavirus is all that more dangerous than other similar viruses is one thing, but that's not what I want to address. Despite whether the coronavirus was a real threat or not, there was, at minimum, a *perceived* threat, and one of the jobs of the president is to make Americans feel like "we're on top of it" so the populace will feel more at ease.

He didn't even do that.

"We have it totally under control. It's one person coming in from China. It's going to be just fine."

This is just one of the shallow things that came out of his mouth about the pandemic. Trump didn't have it under control, and the idea that it was just "one person from China" is another example of his surface-skidding tendencies to trivialize complicated problems with vapid and simple answers that do not mean anything. This is just one example across both his terms in office. Although Trump would claim he was just standing his ground that the coronavirus was nothing to even be worried about, comparing it to a bad flu virus, that wasn't what the people needed to hear, regardless of the situation's severity.

Trump's immigration policies his first term, particularly the separation of families at the United States-Mexico border and the travel bans targeting certain Muslim-majority countries, faced widespread criticism, as they should. He never had an immigration plan other than a wall, and then during his second term, just rounding up a few people that wasted resources and angered a lot of Americans.

During his first run for president, I believe he said something like he was going to build a wall and make Mexico pay for it... okay... explain *how*. I'm a neophyte when it comes to the border, but I do know there are places a wall cannot be built and, more importantly, a lot of that land is privately owned. It would take years and years to secure that land, assuming the people who own it want to sell. If you go with eminent domain, you'll never see a wall in your lifetime.

However, like most promises he made, he stood firm like a rock... which makes total sense because he is about as smart as one.

Let's consider Trump's communication style to solidify this for everyone. His use of social media and controversial statements has been criticized for being a lot of things, including divisive, inflammatory, and, at times, perceived as lacking presidential decorum. I would call most of his social media posts petty and insecure at best, generally obnoxious, and, at worst, downright despicable.

Trump has the likability of a guy smoking a cigar while holding a crying baby as he talks loudly on the phone during a twenty-hour plane flight. And Trump's bullshit goes on and on. From his strained relations with allies through his "America First" approach and international agreements to his responses concerning protests, particularly those related to racial justice, which exacerbated tensions rather than promoting unity.

Now that he's back in office, we have to deal with ICE raids costing millions and achieving very little. Yeah, supporters can say we're rounding up undocumented folks, but you can also clean a floor with a toothbrush and get it as clean as with a mop; it will just take an ungodly amount of time and energy. Not the most effective method, but that's par for the course with this clown.

Also, let's not forget the nightmare of him and the Jeffrey Epstein files, acting like there's nothing to share in the files they have on him. Epstein's accomplice, Ghislaine Maxwell, is in prison for helping the man traffic underage girls. If she was convicted, that means they trafficked people, which means people were serviced. Who are those people? We all know the answer… well, we know at least one answer: Trump.

Beyond all that, we also have to deal with his annoying supporters. At best, they are a bunch of lightly judgmental tight-asses living in their good ol' boy bubble and listening to Jason Aldean, far away from anything or anyone that doesn't fit into their world. These are folks who would name their SUV "Karen" because the SUV they drive is a white Suburban. At worst, his supporters are unforgiving loudmouths that are intolerant of just about anything that goes against their beliefs, particularly on issues related to immigration, race, and LGBTQ+ rights… all of which just contribute to divisions and discrimination.

On top of that, the most extreme of Trump's supporters have a gross kind of love for him. They metaphorically lick his balls every chance they get like some fanboys while promoting conspiracy theories, including claims related to election fraud, deep-state conspiracies, and other unverified or debunked narratives. For the record, I'm not here to denigrate Trump supporters at all… for you Trump supporters, *denigrate* means to put someone down or insult them.

With all that said, Joe Biden might have been worse. It's stunning that anyone could be worse than Trump, but Biden may have achieved that. Not only is he a lying, crooked, dishonest, self-serving, and plagiarizing idiot who never had an original thought in his head, his whole political life has been rooted in just measuring which way the wind is blowing.

For example, he hated Black Americans and homosexuals back in the 1970s and 1980s because it was okay to do so back then, or at least somewhat okay. But now that isn't cool anymore, so he's no longer a racist or a homophobe. Liberals that supported this guy leaned on the cliché go-to line of "People learn and change over time," but that's not true in Biden's case... and even those folks know it.

To be fair, I don't believe he's racist or homophobic anymore, but that's not because he's changed. I don't think he knows what planet he's on, let alone has enough brain cells left to remember how racist and homophobic he actually is. But none of this should come as any surprise. He's been a total fraud since he entered public office. When he ran for president back in the 1980s, he lifted whole parts of other people's speeches and thought no one would figure it out. These weren't obscure folks. This dude lifted whole parts from John F. Kennedy, Robert Kennedy, and Neil Kinnock.

It's like me recording Michael Jackson's *Thriller* and passing it off as my own song, thinking no one is going to recognize it. The level of his stupidity is so off the charts, it goes beyond sad and actually becomes quite fascinating... it's like asking, "How much stupider could you possibly be?" The answer: "None more stupider." Joe Biden has spent his entire career climbing the Mt. Everest of stupid over and over again, reaching the peak every time. And this was in the 1980s when he actually still had a brain in his head that didn't resemble a piñata at the end of a birthday party.

The point is this: This guy would say *anything* to get elected… including the things other people have said.

That's even before we start with his record as president, which included such gems as the disastrous withdrawal from Afghanistan, inflation, massive government spending, supply chain problems, and the biggest issue that kept plaguing him: his border security and immigration policy. Well, to be fair, you cannot really criticize his border policy because he doesn't seem to have one.

He's the only man to ever make America easier to get into than a public school. Again… the incompetence is so off the chart, it actually becomes fascinating to see.

And what did Biden have to say about this?

"We'll teach Donald Trump ahhh ahh vuuwable lesson. Don't mess with mmmmedle America unless you wanna get the benefit. And by the way… use to make brew beered here, errhhh ahhh, easy it's make beer brew… errrr… brew…"

What the fuck did you say? I feel like I need the decoder ring Ralphie had in *A Christmas Story*.

Criticism regarding Biden's mental abilities had been a topic of discussion since he took office, and he never failed to disappoint. If it wasn't verbal slip-ups, it was flat-out incoherent statements or mumbling, or him claiming to have just talked with someone who died a decade ago. On top of that, he had dozens of instances where he appeared to forget major details about his own personal life, like not knowing when he served as vice president or when his son died. This dude even made the basic task of walking off a stage look like someone stuck in the middle of a cornfield maze.

It was hard to argue that all of these moments combined shouldn't have raised concerns about his cognitive abilities, which they did among Republicans. The White House just blew them off while Harris defended Biden's competency... until the first debate happened. We all remember that glorious meeting of the minds. Every time either one of them opened their mouth, George Washington rolled over in his grave. By the end of the debate, Washington probably just looked like a rotisserie chicken spinning nonstop. Suddenly the Democrats wanted Biden out and seemingly were the only ones surprised that Biden might have some cognitive issues. Really? Even Stevie Wonder could see it. For Christ's sakes, at the time of his inauguration in 2021, Biden was the oldest person ever to assume the office of the U.S. presidency... and this is the same man who was a walking tree stump when he was in his forties over four decades earlier.

However, at the time, a lot of people thought it was a blessing in disguise. Biden is out, and now the constituents can select someone else at the national convention. Ideally, that someone wouldn't be the political equivalent of the fifth member of

O-Town. Remember O-Town? Of course you don't. Well, that didn't happen. The Democratic National Committee just inserted Harris unilaterally. You got the political equivalent of the fourth member of O-Town. Congratulations.

From the moment Kamala Harris launched her presidential campaign, she never managed to define herself clearly to voters, with the absence of a clear political identity. She was dogged by her inability to articulate any platform, that cackle that frightened children, and a truly inauthentic personality, which was about as genuine as Taco Bell, the only border she probably ever went to visit. The national stage didn't work for her. Her answers to almost every question were nonsensical streams of clichés and word salads that I envision is what a box of wine would sound like if it could talk. It was like a lengthy Hallmark card. On one hand, it sounded positive, but on the other hand, it didn't really say anything or mean anything. After watching what looked like *Weekend at Bernie's 3* for several months, the DNC got rid of that corpse and pushed this block of Velveeta into our faces.

So, when folks came up to me and said I was throwing my vote away by supporting a third party, I just smirked.

"You're voting for either Trump or Biden, then Harris, and you think *I'm* the one throwing my vote away?"

Nonetheless, I get why they feel this way. Folks think that all third-party voters are doing this because they feel disillusioned or dissatisfied with the major political parties' platforms or failures to follow through. They believe that all of us just perceive the two-party system as failing to represent our values or address critical issues, and that's the sole reason we're voting for a third party… and this is mostly true… at least that was the main issue in the past. Now the main concern from us is this shit-show of candidates. Both major parties continue to give us political and ideologically intolerant clowns completely unfit for the office of the presidency, and we demand these two parties simply do better. If inadequate and incapable were a car, Biden and Trump would be arguing with each other over who is going to drive and who is sitting shotgun.

For third-party voters, there is some nuance here. If a third-party candidate better aligns with one's specific policy preferences, they're going to vote for them regardless. Nonetheless, I believe that today most people cast their ballots for third-party candidates more as a form of protest against the choices offered by the major parties. Still, we third-party supporters get the same reaction every time: "You cannot win, so you're just throwing your vote away."

Again, let me make this clear: We're not trying to win the election… we just want to fuck *your* candidate over.

But why do we want to do that? How does that help?

Well, it's the only way we can get these two parties to start doing better. Third parties can't win, but we can derail your chances. Maybe if both major parties continually fear that possibility, they'll start actually nominating candidates that aren't the equivalent of a bag of flaming dog shit on your porch and start doing the job of effectively governing and representing the people… maybe they will stop treating Americans like cattle or like powerless children they can stand over, telling us that "you have to take what we give you and you will like it."

At the end of the day, someone has to lose in an election… and despite third parties' chances of winning being absolutely zero, we're not the ones losing… they are… and if we can actually force the two major parties to do better, we won. It's kind of ironic, isn't it?

# A Third-Party Voter Explains Why Kamala Harris Lost So Badly

When I cast my choice for President of the United States, I knew my candidate had no chance. The same was true for Kamala Harris… unfortunately for her supporters, they didn't know that. In fact, they were optimistic. No fault of theirs. They should have been optimistic. By all metrics, this election was going to be very close. That didn't happen. Harris not only lost, she was crushed by a landslide and didn't win even one swing state. It wasn't close or even competitive by any measure. She lost the Electoral College, the popular vote, and Republicans took seats in the House and Senate.

But why? What happened?

I watched this election unfold until the early morning hours when Donald J. Trump was declared the winner. I saw the polls move, the votes come in, and the pundits on both sides of the aisle twist and manipulate the narratives throughout the night. As an independent observer, it became painfully clear to me why Harris not only lost, but why she lost so badly.

There are three primary reasons this campaign failed.

One: Identity politics doesn't work and, in fact, works against you.

This is the primary reason she lost. The Democrats made a huge mistake not only by overestimating how well identity politics would play, but by failing to even consider if this approach could actually hurt them… and it did. Badly. For Harris, her entire campaign was centered on identity politics… this idea that the majority of the country would rally around political alliances based on ethnic groups, race, gender, socio-economic status, and social background rather than traditional broad-based party politics. This move not only didn't help galvanize the population at large, but the demonization of the population that didn't join this identity-driven political movement actually alienated and upset many more Americans than the Democrats ever thought it would.

This election's result sent a clear message: Identity politics doesn't work. The Democrats failed to recognize the firestorm they were fully embracing. Fact of the matter is this: Average Joe American, who is treading water every day just to make ends meet under this country's outrageous inflation and struggling economy, is tired of being called a misogynist, LGBTQ+-phobe, racist, and neo-Nazi. They are tired of being told to shut up and that their opinion doesn't matter. While the Democrats accurately predicted that all misogynists, LGBTQ+-phobes, racists, and neo-Nazis would vote for Trump, they failed to understand that 98% of people who voted for Trump (or considered it) are not any of these things.

Harris failed to recognize that these folks are fed up with being condescended to and treated like they're all hate-filled malcontents and the cause of all the ills of others while, at the same time, struggling to eke out a decent life for themselves and their family in an economy that was rapidly working against them.

Two: No one asked for Harris, while many asked for Trump.

In a two-party system like America's, many feel trapped… that they have no choice but to vote for one or the other. I'm that exception, but I'm clearly the minority. For most everyone else, they will choose one or the other. This choice comes down to three basic formulas that ultimately dictate who one votes for. They are as follows:

1.) I don't care who Candidate A is, I will never vote for Candidate B: This is your stereotypical party die-hard. They will vote Democrat or Republican every time, all the time, regardless.

2.) I like Candidate A, I don't like Candidate B: This is your more independent voter who likely is registered with one of the major parties but can change their vote. They vote for someone because of the current climate in America, the economy, ever-evolving social and cultural shifts, larger geopolitical issues at hand, and/or the policies and approaches of a given candidate during a given time period. They are not party loyalists.

3.) I hate both Candidate A and B, so I'll vote for the one I hate the least: This is the classic "lesser of two evils" vote.

Harris was put in an unfavorable situation because the reality is this: No one asked for Harris, but a lot of folks asked for Trump. She was behind the 8-ball from the start. Trump would secure votes from party loyalists, votes from people that saw him as "the lesser of two evils," and, most importantly, people who liked his policies and approach to current issues they felt were important to America. Harris, on the other hand, only had votes coming from party loyalists and those who saw her as "the lesser of two evils." No one actually asked for Harris, and her inability to explain her policies didn't attract anyone to vote for her based on policies. She never gave anyone a reason to ask for her. Again, her campaign was almost all identity politics. Considering that political independents constitute the largest political bloc in the U.S., with an average of 43% of U.S. adults identifying this way in 2023, according to Gallup, what reasons did she give to convince anyone to ask for her?

Three: The DNC's recent patterns of shamelessly and unabashedly screwing over their constituents.

For the record, the GOP is not innocent. They do this too. However, the degree and the recency of the Democrats doing this put a huge negative spotlight on them. In 2016, Bernie Sanders looked poised to take the Democratic nomination for president... until the DNC made sure Hillary Clinton won. They openly and unapologetically undermined the wishes of their own constituents. In 2024, they decided to not only double-down, they tripled-down, and then quadrupled-down.

First, they doubled-down by hiding the fact that President Joe Biden was suffering a significant mental decline, telling everyone that he was the sharpest man in the room... then a debate happened and we all learned that he wasn't the sharpest man in the room. Within minutes following that debate, Democrats tripled-down by calling for him to step aside, suddenly ignoring the years of defending his mental acuity, thus insulting their constituents' intelligence by gaslighting them to believe they never defended Biden. Then they quadrupled-down by unilaterally inserting Harris rather than letting the folks at the convention have any say in Biden's replacement. This was a major "fuck you" and it alienated a lot of voters.

Harris' campaign was likely doomed before it was even launched, and she made a major misstep by unknowingly sabotaging herself further by centering her whole campaign on identity politics. It didn't work… and looking at the post--election coverage, it seems the Democrats still haven't figured this out, as they continue to lean into identity politics, smashing Americans who voted for Trump as misogynists, LGBTQ+-phobes, racists, and neo-Nazis who didn't want a Black woman as president, opting to willingly vote for a Hitler-esque fascist dictator in Trump.

At the end of the day, Harris could have pivoted and won. She could have salvaged the negative impact the party's open disregard for their constituents, and her own unearned nomination, had on her campaign. She could have done this by focusing on issues that the majority of Americans care about. However, instead of talking about how to fix the problems, she focused on how many Americans are the problem that needs to be fixed.

# Hashtag Revolution: The Slacktivisim of American Youth

In a world teetering on the brink of collapse, be it environmental, political, spiritual, or one's Wi-Fi, there stands a new generation of warriors: slacktivists. They are armed with smartphones, curated playlists, and more opinions than experience. They are passionate, powerful, and permanently online.

Now, these folks are not to be confused with actual activists who sweat, organize, and often smell like protest and injustice. Slacktivists are a special breed of young Americans who have discovered that changing the world doesn't require leaving the couch, just a decent Wi-Fi connection and a Canva subscription. Slacktivism is the noble art of appearing woke while staying conveniently seated. Why would you rally in the streets when you can rally in the comments? Why organize a protest when you can post a quote by Angela Davis over a picture of a sunset and call it a day?

It's the glittering, echo-chambered world of modern American youth, where vibes matter more than votes and engagement is more urgent than actual engagement.

This is the hashtag generation… the generation that still doesn't know it's called a pound sign. Maybe if we had a rally protesting the erasure of the pound sign and made that viral, slacktivists would learn that fact. It seems to be the only time slacktivists take notice of anything. It all begins with a scroll in the morning before teeth are brushed or existential dread is fully digested. Young Americans open their phones to learn which new tragedy, injustice, or geopolitical conflict they'll be standing in solidarity with from afar.

They stand with Palestine, then Ukraine, scrolling down to learn that they also stand with Britney, then start posting their own passionate support for... wait... what's the trending hashtag again?

The sentiment is sincere... sort of... but it's also fleeting. The issue of the day burns bright, gets an Instagram story with the right font and filter, and then vanishes once another issue takes center stage or Starbucks drops a new seasonal drink. These youth activists are quick to show support but not quite as quick to do the boring parts... you know, the research, voting in local elections, donating consistently, or reading beyond the first paragraph of a Vox explainer. They will, however, make an infographic with perfect color contrast to explain "the situation" in 10 pastel slides. That counts, right?

Slacktivists love online petitions the way boomers love forwarding conspiracy-laced emails. If there's a cause worth caring about, there's a petition with 400,000 signatures that no one with any real power or influence cares about. Change.org has become the church of the slacktivist. It doesn't matter if the petition is addressed to "The Government" or "The People In Charge," what matters is that it was shared, preferably with fire emojis and all-caps captions like "DO BETTER." As I said, these petitions often go ignored by actual institutions, but in the world of slacktivism, it's the gesture that counts. Like putting "thoughts and prayers" in Helvetica Bold.

The revolution will not be televised… but it will be online. For some, it's the only place where it happens. Yes, nothing screams "revolution" quite like a downloadable protest toolkit in pastel tones. Slacktivists are nothing if not aesthetically invested, and their activism must match the feed. Rage, yes… but it has to be on brand. Modern activism looks good now. You can express moral outrage and still keep your grid cohesive. You can demand justice but do so without using red, because red clashes with your current Instagram aesthetic. It's social justice optimized for social media.

Gone are the days when you had to brave the elements to demand change. The youth of today know you can fight injustice from your bed, in fuzzy socks, with snacks. Why risk tear gas when you can watch someone else protest live on TikTok and leave a comment that says "Yesss queen!" or "This is what we need!" If you're feeling extra brave, you might even livestream yourself watching them livestream. It's protest inception. Layers upon layers of passive support, like a justice-flavored lasagna. And if the protest doesn't align with your brand? Easy fix. Just repost someone else's video with a caption that says "Signal Boosting." It's like being there, but with less effort and better lighting.

This is just a glorified version of clicktivism, the act of pretending digital engagement is equivalent to real-world action. A generation raised on dopamine hits now believes that every "like" is a lifeline, every "share" a sacrifice. They'll proudly let us know that every like is a punch to the face of oppression. Every retweet is a blow against tyranny. Every heart emoji under a sad story is practically a policy initiative.

Of course, nothing changes, but that's beside the point. The algorithm rewards emotional participation, not actual impact. As long as you're trending, you're doing something… right?

Modern youth don't just care. They curate their caring.

They'll fight for women's rights, unless it's women in countries not trending this week. They'll call out racism, unless it interferes with their favorite celebrity's brand partnership. They'll repost information about the climate crisis, unless it means they have to cancel that flight to Coachella.

Slacktivism is all about convenient conviction. It's caring within boundaries. Passionate, but practical. Furious, but flexible. It's social justice, but make it manageable. This selectiveness is not always intentional, just algorithmic. Social media rewards novelty and hot takes, not long-term engagement or consistency. So the slacktivist passion burns hot… until something shinier arrives.

At its core, slacktivism is performative. And no performance is complete without applause. Without the affirmation that virtue signaling brings, what would be the point? Social justice? Change?

Equality? Yeah, those things are cool and all of that, but the act of expressing your woke opinions needs to also demonstrate that you *have* them. It's activism as self-branding. It's not about doing the right thing. It's about being seen doing the right thing. Young Americans will proudly announce they're "educating themselves" on an issue, then link to a Wikipedia article they skimmed. They'll post a black square on Instagram, then go right back to brunch. They'll make a TikTok explaining systemic oppression while dancing to Megan Thee Stallion. It's activism with a ring light and a revolution that fits in your story highlights.

Interestingly, slacktivists are also tired. Exhausted, really. Despite doing very little in practice, they are spiritually and emotionally burnt out from the *idea* of activism. Who can blame them? Every day brings a new tragedy. A new outrage. A new call to action that must be honored with a vague, emotional repost. This constant emotional cycling leads to performative burnout, where people announce they're "logging off for self-care," only to return six hours later with a new infographic about climate grief and a smoothie.

Slacktivism may not change the world, but it feels like a lot of work. And feelings, as we know, are everything.

Deep down, slacktivists believe in change. They really do. They just believe that someone else will be the one to actually make it happen. They are the moral cheerleaders, waving digital pom-poms while others do the heavy lifting. They might show up to vote, if it's convenient, and if the ballot isn't too confusing. But they won't canvass, won't organize, and won't challenge power in any sustained way. Why is this? Because true activism is messy, slow, frustrating, and often thankless. It rarely fits neatly in an Instagram story. It doesn't trend.

So they slack on, armed with vibes, confident that they're on the right side of history… even if they're not moving. Slacktivism is the illusion of impact… the theater of justice. While it's easy to mock, it's also important to remember why it exists. Young Americans didn't invent broken systems. They inherited them. And in a world that often feels too big, too corrupt, and too chaotic, the impulse to do something, anything, even digitally, is understandable. However, if slacktivism is the beginning, it can't be the end. The world won't be saved by hashtags. No infographic has ever dismantled oppression. And change doesn't come from good vibes… it comes from good work.

So, yes, share that post. Sign that petition. Raise that awareness… but after that, close the app. Step outside. Show up. Always remember: if the revolution is livestreamed, someone still has to plug in the cord.

# Redistribution 101: Leftist Students Meet Grade Equality

In the hallowed halls of academia, where dreams are shaped, caffeine is worshipped, and Wi-Fi is a human right, there exists the modern anti-capitalist student. These young crusaders don the Che Guevara shirts fresh from the thrift store, sip $7 organic oat milk lattes, and rail against the horrors of capitalism from the safety of a classroom that taxpayers paid for. They are passionate. They are loud. They are absolutely, unwaveringly committed to dismantling the systems of oppression that have led to the psychological trauma of not getting Coachella tickets during pre-sale.

Their enemy? Capitalism. Their motto? "Eat the rich!" Their anthem? Something by Rage Against the Machine, but only on vinyl, of course.

While the most fascinating moments in the young anti-capitalist's journey usually occur during a protest or while angrily retweeting Elon Musk memes, this wouldn't be the case for 35 students in one of my college English classes. For these young defenders of equality, the most fascinating moment happened when I decided to practice what these students preach: redistributing grades.

It was a microcosm of ideology meeting reality. A true Marxist moment, right there in my English class.

It started like any other semester. Students trickled into my class wearing hoodies that said "Late Stage Capitalism Is Killing Me," armed with Hydro Flasks and the unearned confidence of people who skimmed *The Communist Manifesto* between Netflix episodes. I have always had a passion for both theory and mild chaos, and I had grown weary of hearing the same tired slogans.

"Capitalism is a pyramid scheme!"

"Money is a social construct!"

"I shouldn't have to pay rent, for Christ's sake… it's 2025!"

Of course, the class started off somewhat normal, but as the kids became more comfortable with me, they started questioning the readings we were doing. Specifically, Ayn Rand's *Atlas Shrugged*, a book they found particularly problematic due to its capitalistic leanings. I had grown tired of this semester after semester, so, in a flash of mischievousness, I made an announcement that would change everything.

"Starting this week, we will be distributing grades equally across the class. Those of you who have A's will have a portion of your points redistributed to those who are failing, so that we can ensure grade equity. After all, we're building a fairer classroom together, aren't we?"

You could hear the iPhones drop.

At first, the room was silent. Not out of shock… keep in mind these were students who routinely participated in "silent protests." That wasn't the reason this time. This time, it was out of sheer confusion. A brave soul named Madison raised her hand and spoke up. Madison was a devout anti-capitalist who, in high school, once wore a "Tax Jeff Bezos" shirt to her father's job site during a "take your kid to work day." He worked at Amazon.

"Wait... like... are you serious?"

I nodded.

"Quite serious. You all value equity over competition, yes? We are implementing a redistribution model. Everyone should benefit equally, regardless of input or effort."

Another student, Ethan, chimed in.

"But I studied, like, all weekend for that last test we took."

"Exactly," I said with a smile. "And your efforts will now uplift others. Isn't that the foundation of collective success?"

A murmur rippled through the classroom. Eyes darted. Discord servers lit up. Suddenly, the socialist utopia didn't feel so utopian.

By the following week, the first redistribution had occurred. High-achieving students watched their 94% dip to 85%, while others with 55% saw miraculous bumps to passing grades. There was no curve, only justice... the kind you post about in Instagram carousels, not the kind you want on your transcript.

A lot of folks in class weren't too happy. Jacob, who had built his academic brand on having a 4.0 and casually mentioning it in group projects, was inconsolable.

"This is grade theft," he declared on his Finsta. "I literally earned that A."

His post was met with a few supportive comments and one anonymous reply: "Sounds like capitalist propaganda, bro."

Meanwhile, Sasha, who had spent most of the semester reading fanfiction in the back row, was thrilled.

"I feel seen," she said. "I shouldn't be punished just because traditional learning structures don't align with my vibe."

Her grade jumped from 59% to 75%. She celebrated with a TikTok titled "Unlearning Capitalist Constructs of Academic Hierarchy."

It got 24,000 likes.

Nowhere was my new system more controversial than during group projects. Traditionally, students hated them because someone always did all the work while someone else coasted. But under the new redistribution model, coasting was institutionalized.

"Guys," said Carlos, a former lower-end A student now teetering on the edge of academic ruin with a constant C grade due to distribution, "shouldn't we all just put in the same amount of effort?"

"Why?" said Brianna, who hadn't opened the syllabus since January. "Isn't this, like, the definition of mutual aid?"

"No," Carlos groaned. "This is the definition of me doing everything while you vibe."

The tension was palpable. Slack messages turned passive-aggressive. Shared Google Docs became battlegrounds. The line between social justice and academic self-interest blurred faster than a political candidate in an election year. By mid-semester, my office hours were less about help and more about heated debates.

"I'm all for equality," one student said, "but not when it comes to my grade."

"So you're fine with redistributing wealth, but not academic success?" I asked.

"Well, yeah, because like… grades are earned. You know?"

"Ah," I said, pretending to take notes. "So some merit is okay, as long as it benefits you?"

The student stormed out, muttering something about "nuance."

Outside of class, students continued their digital activism. The class Slack group was flooded with posts calling the redistribution policy "harmful," "toxic," and "academic violence." A Change.org petition was launched titled "Stop the Grade Inequality Masquerading as Equality." Ironically, these were the same students who, just weeks before, had rallied against academic competition and called for systemic reform.

The hypocrisy wasn't subtle. One particularly vocal student tweeted:

"Grades are just a number. We must abolish the GPA-industrial complex."

But when that same student's 97% dropped to an 81%, they posted again:

"This is an attack on high-achievers. Academic discrimination is real."

Turns out, even the most passionate anti-capitalists have their limits, especially when Dean's List eligibility is at stake. Eventually, I revealed the truth: the redistribution was a temporary lesson, a simulation to spark critical thinking about economic models and personal values.

"You've all been living out your own socialist utopia," I announced. "How does it feel?"

There was silence. A few groans.

However, something magical happened. The students, now faced with the gap between ideology and personal interest, began to reflect. They discussed the complexity of fairness, the role of incentives, the difference between equality and equity. It was messy, uncomfortable, and, ironically, the best lesson of the semester. Once normal grading resumed, the class returned to its natural order. The overachievers rejoiced. The underachievers resumed blaming the system, but something had changed. When the next debate about capitalism arose, the students spoke with a little more nuance, a little less certainty, and a little more humility. They still hated capitalism, but now they understood why some people cling to it, especially when grades, bonuses, or triple-shot espressos are involved.

Modern young people are not stupid. They're idealistic, opinionated, and trying to make sense of a broken world. Their critique of capitalism is rooted in real problems: inequality, exploitation, burnout, and the terrifying price of avocado toast. My experiment didn't solve these issues; it just revealed a simple fact: It's easy to advocate for redistribution until it costs you something. Everyone wants equality, in theory. However, when equality touches their GPA or paycheck, the tone shifts real fast. The lesson isn't that young people are hypocrites. It's that ideology, like group projects, gets complicated when humans are involved. When fairness conflicts with self-interest, the real beliefs bubble up.

So the next time a student tweets "abolish capitalism," check their GPA. If it's a 4.0, they might just mean "abolish capitalism… for other people." At the end of the day, who can blame them? After all, revolution is fun… until someone takes your A.

# Doomsday Cultists: The End of Days That Never Seems to End

It's the end of the world as we know it… and I feel fine. In 2025, several well-known psychics came together and proclaimed the world would end before the final stroke of midnight on December 31st. This caught some national attention, although I do not know exactly why. Yes, a few "well-known" psychics predicted the end of the world, but that has been going on for hundreds, if not thousands, of years. Nothing is different, including the reaction from doomsday cultists. Even though every other "end of the world" failed to manifest, they are claiming, for a 100 percent fact, this is the one that will… just as every other before it was the one.

The trouble with doomsday cultists is that they keep predicting the end of the world but never provide snacks for the waiting period. Nor do they provide the popcorn for us when the sun rises just in time to see the disappointment on their faces.

In 2023, two mid-sized banks, Silicon Valley Bank and Signature Bank, collapsed. While this should have had everyone at least a bit concerned, it wasn't the spark of total global financial failure that would have completely disintegrated our society. However, we can always count on the doomsday cultists to proclaim that the world will soon be a *Mad Max* film, and they lost their collective shit when these two banks went down, proclaiming it was the beginning of the end. Well… it's 2026. Looks like you need to go back to whatever biblical scripture or star-gazing you do to figure out your miscalculation. Let's face it… it's the doomsday cultists' world, and we are all just living in it.

While it's true that the failure of Silicon Valley Bank and Signature Bank was going to have a serious impact on the economy, and we all should be aware of that when these types of situations happen, it didn't spell the end of the world. However, doomsday cultists said different, despite the fact that 24 hours before these collapses came to light, most of these idiots had never even heard of these banks.

For doomsday cultists, don't act like you're familiar with these banks or have some stake in this game. You're all freaked out because two banks you've never heard of are now bankrupt? What are you going to do when mega-investment firm Holloway Evergreen Global Investments files for bankruptcy next week? I know what you'll do. You'll lose your shit, buy a year's supply of munitions, buy a solar-powered generator, and tune into Coast to Coast radio to get updates on how this latest collapse is connected to that child-trafficking pizza shop and how the death of… well… anyone who's died recently is tied to the Clintons. Just pick a name. It doesn't matter… and they've never even heard of Holloway Evergreen Global Investments, but their insolvency is freaking the doomsday cultists out as they read this. They probably think this collapse will be the one that totally dooms us.

I'll save you a Google search: Holloway Evergreen Global Investments is not filing for bankruptcy next week. There is nothing wrong with the company, nor are they headed for any financial ruin with investors' money being lost... and that's not because they are on solid ground with a history of smart and strategic safe investing practices. It's because they don't exist. I just made them up right now.

See how freaked out these jackasses just got over an imaginary company?

Look, I'm here to ease the fears of doomsday cultists. I have a long history of investing and consider myself a guru, of sorts, when it comes to safely investing. I have a failsafe way to secure your money. This practice is ironclad, and no matter which banks fail, big or small, or how many of them fail, you will never lose a dime of your money.

Stick that shit under the fucking mattress.

FTX, cryptocurrency, banks, stocks, corporations, bonds, ETFs, REITs... forget about all of that shit. Under the fucking mattress is untouchable. Still unsure? Let me take you to school.

Look at every stock exchange on this planet. Do you see "Sean R. Cabibi's Mattress" listed on any exchange? No, you don't. Look up every bank in this country. Did you find "Sean's Mattress and Trust" anywhere? Nope... you didn't find shit. Can't lose your money if the place where you have it invested cannot collapse. The mattress has been 100% undefeated during every known economic collapse. Most folks can't even fathom the security the mattress provides, but the doomsday cultists will get it. Y'all sheep are playing checkers while the rest of us are playing chess.

Now, I know what you're thinking. I just told you it's under the mattress. It's no longer secure. Sike, bitches! It's actually *in* the mattress. Doomsday cultists are always five steps ahead of you.

Wait, didn't I just expose its location again?

Maybe I did… maybe I didn't.

Maybe I'm doing what Minister D did in Edgar Allan Poe's story *The Purloined Letter*. I'll leave all my money out in plain sight. You see, that's so obvious, you'll never look there, and thus, never find it. Maybe it's sitting on a table right in front of you. Maybe it's actually still under my mattress. Maybe it's in the mattress. Maybe I don't own a mattress, just a foldout sofa… which still has a mattress in it. It's all mind games at this point, and doomsday folks are living rent-free in your head right now. Maybe you've never read Edgar Allan Poe or *The Purloined Letter* and have no clue what I'm talking about. Well, read some classic literature instead of inflammatory news about banks collapsing and the end of the world as we know it.

It's the same with climate change. The doomsday cultists gargle the proverbial nuts of that apocalyptic wet dream. Look, just because a tornado happens, or a hurricane comes through, or some snowstorm buries your city, it's not necessarily because of climate change. It's not a sign that the end of days is coming. Those things have been happening since the dawn of time.

Oh, it's the frequency and severity of the storms that you're talking about? Look, most of the country gets a ton of severe weather all the time, and has for centuries. You don't like it? Move to California where I live. Sure, every few years we get an earthquake that might rattle your cage, but that's it... and I don't want to hear about the recent California storms as some clear proof of climate change either. Yeah, shit like this happens in California every few decades. In a few weeks we'll be back to endless sunshine while you doomsday cultists will again tie yourselves to a tree, praying that you survive whatever storm is about to pummel your trailer park.

Good news is this: Nothing lasts forever, so you can come back to this essay in 30 years when another tornado strikes California and tell us all that the world is ending… assuming you didn't die in one of the thousands of hurricanes, snowstorms, floods, or tornadoes you'll be facing during that time… or from the never-ending poverty or bad batches of moonshine you brewed in your tub.

Bottom line: The economy isn't collapsing, the climate does weird shit all the time, lizard people don't exist, the Illuminati isn't real, no one is trying to send you hidden messages buried in the text of blogs, and severe weather in California does happen sometimes. Now, if you'll excuse me, I have to put on a slightly heavier jacket than normal before I head out to work.

# Screaming Viking: The Origins of the Infamous *Cheers* Cocktail

"Would you like the cucumber bruised?"

That was the question Woody Boyd asked Norm Peterson on September 24, 1987. I was 13 at the time, and *Cheers* was my favorite television show. It still is today. The show had such a profound effect on me. In my early 20s, I pursued the dream of one day owning a bar. I worked in journalism and teaching, but ultimately used those jobs to finance the dream. Today I own a bar, as well as other real estate holdings. I also brew my own beer.

While the entire series of *Cheers* was crucial in my life's journey, this season-six premiere episode would ultimately play a role in my desire to learn more about mixology and the process of brewing beer. It also led me and my bartender, Martika, one night in 1998, to attempt to make a Screaming Viking, the infamous drink that appeared in that episode.

Here's the story, if you need a refresher on this *Cheers* episode. At this point in the series, Sam Malone has sold Cheers and is no longer the owner. He returns to the bar and asks Rebecca Howe, the new manager of Cheers, for a job as a bartender. She informs him that they have all the bartenders they need and are not hiring. When Rebecca's boss finds out that the former Boston Red Sox pitcher Sam Malone wants a job, he is adamant that she fire someone and get Sam on staff. He's hired, but Sam realizes that Woody is likely the one who will be fired soon because Rebecca wouldn't fire the guy she hired, Wayne, a genius bartender who can make any drink in existence.

To prevent Woody from getting fired, the Cheers regulars devise a plan. They challenge the arrogant Wayne, questioning his ability to make every drink known to man, and bet him that someone would come into the bar that night and order a drink he doesn't know how to make.

"Impossible, I know every drink there is…" says Wayne.

But if that happens, Wayne would have to quit the job and let Sam take his spot. He agrees, overly confident that this will never happen.

Eventually Norm strolls in, having not been to Cheers since Sam left and now virtually unknown at the bar, other than to hardcore regulars who are in on the scam. Norm sits down, and Wayne asks him what he would like to drink.

"I'll have a Screaming Viking."

Wayne attempts to correct him and begins arguing that there is no such drink. Suddenly, Woody comes into frame and addresses Norm.

"Would you like the cucumber bruised?"

"Slightly," Norm says.

Out of nowhere, other patrons who are in on the scam begin ordering Screaming Vikings. This overwhelms and angers

Wayne, who quits and storms out. Rebecca, who finds all of this very odd, asks to see Sam in her office. Everyone who ordered the drink makes a toast and takes a swig. As Rebecca stares at them suspiciously, she walks into her office with Sam and shuts the door. The entire bar spits out whatever it was that was served to them.

As a kid, I assumed that most every drink had already been created to some degree because only certain things can be mixed together. My 13-year-old brain saw the episode and came to the conclusion that Woody had to mix liquors and mixers together that didn't work... because if he mixed ones that did, it would be identified as an existing drink, blowing their plan apart. This is why they all spit it out. What I learned later on in life is that it's not that simple and, in fact, just reinforced the fact that it's a television show... nothing is real. The drink doesn't exist.

As an adult in the mid-1990s, I became somewhat enamored with mixology and brewing. Being more of a beer guy, I started drifting toward brewing beer, learning all the different ways you can create beer with limitless flavors and profiles. This episode, as well as another episode of *Cheers* where Woody attempts to create a brand-new drink, always inspired me to study the process and the complex art of brewing and mixology.

In 1998, I bought my first bar. One night, just a few weeks after purchasing the establishment, I made the joke to my bartender, Martika, when she asked what I wanted to drink. I said, "A

Screaming Viking, cucumber slightly bruised." She didn't get it, but two other patrons at the bar laughed, understanding the reference.

I explained the joke to Martika. She looked at me and asked if I remembered what was in the drink. She wanted to know what I recalled from the episode, if anything at all. There was no real Internet at the time, so we couldn't watch the clip from the show, and there was no existing recipe we could find online in 1998. The World Wide Web was still in its infancy.

What were we going to do? We certainly couldn't call the alcoholics' helpline and ask, "How do you make a Screaming Viking?"

Ironically, much like Wayne from the episode, Martika was highly skilled in spirits... not only in understanding tastes and aromas, but also in the history and origins of liquors, how to mix just about anything, and to what degree things would have to be balanced to create certain flavors and profiles.

All we had was the very limited info from the show.

We knew the drink had a cucumber garnish. I also remembered that the glass Norm had contained clear liquor, not brown or any other color that would indicate certain liquors or mixers. That was all we had to go on. There were no other shots in the episode showing anything that would indicate what was in a Screaming Viking.

Martika started with the name "Screaming Viking," assuming the drink might originate from the Nordic region.

I suggested that the main liquor be vodka because Norm's drink was clear, and vodka seemed more Nordic to me than any other clear liquor, like gin. She said that the Scandinavian countries have liquor called aquavit, which is very similar to vodka since it's made from potatoes, but also distilled with herbs like dill and caraway. If a Screaming Viking did exist and originated from that region, they would have used aquavit over vodka. We didn't have aquavit in the bar, but after a few calls to other local establishments, we found a bottle, and the owner was gracious enough to have someone bring it to us.

At this point, Martika had to make some unfounded calls about the drink. Everything from here on out would be a complete guess. It was a clear-based drink garnished with a cucumber. That's all we had to go on. She decided the best route was to keep things standard but try to add flavors that would make it distinctive, focusing on ingredients from the Nordic region whenever possible. She decided to add dry vermouth, ultimately mimicking the recipe of a Cucumber Vodka Martini, which is a classic drink.

But here is where it got complicated: What we had now was a Cucumber Vodka Martini, just with a different base liquor, not vodka, but something very close to it. At this point, we could have said it was done, but Martika said she wanted it to be different than just a martini. It had to be its own thing.

Martika thought of adding absinthe because of its origins in Switzerland, close to the Nordic region, and because it had an understated black licorice flavor that wouldn't contrast too hard with the cucumber, making the Screaming Viking similar to a Black Licorice Widow Martini, but with a much more discreet licorice flavor. Black Licorice Widows typically use Sambuca or Jägermeister, both of which have far more powerful black licorice flavors. Absinthe also has a much stronger lore behind it because of its controversy. This would make the Screaming Viking much more intriguing. The problem was that at that time, absinthe was not legal in America. Our bar did have bottles of Sambuca, Jägermeister, and a bottle of Pernod Anise. She went with the anise because its flavor is closest to absinthe and it is made from anise, versus the others that only use anise as part of their process.

Martika took this combination and mixed various amounts of the ingredients until we both agreed on the final recipe. She decided to add orange bitters to slightly offset the sweetness of the anise.

It was done. All hail the Screaming Viking.

We added the drink to our menu, even putting up a framed poster of the scene in *Cheers* where Norm orders the drink with the caption, "I'll have a Screaming Viking."

As far as I can tell, we were the first bar in America to serve a Screaming Viking and make it a mainstay on our drink menu.

It was moderately popular, especially with guests who were fans of the show. However, in 2007, when the United States legalized absinthe, the drink saw a huge jump, as we offered the drink with either anise or absinthe.

Today, you can find drink recipes for a Screaming Viking all over the Internet that are similar to Martika's, as well as ones that have zero similarities to what she created. It begs the question: Did Martika invent this drink in 1998? Well, maybe… I'm not sure if there is a bar anywhere that was serving this drink, or any variation of it, before 1998. Today, the drink remains a staple of my bar. Martika has moved on and now owns her own tavern. Surprisingly, she doesn't have a Screaming Viking on her menu but will make it if you ask.

Over the years, the Internet has put the Screaming Viking on the map with hundreds of recipes, but Martika is still referred to as "the creator of the Screaming Viking" around our city. While never getting national attention for any of this, every once in a while she'll have media outlets contact her for various interviews, especially if anything surrounding *Cheers* comes back into the news, such as anniversaries and the like. She always responds the same way when asked about inventing the drink. She says she didn't invent anything… Woody Boyd did. She just helped work out the fine details.

Here is the recipe:

- 2 oz Aquavit
- 1/2 oz Dry Vermouth

- 1/2 oz Pernod Anise or Absinthe

- 2 dashes of Orange Bitters

- Ice

- Cucumber slice for garnish

Instructions:

Chill the glass: Start by chilling a cocktail glass. You can do this by filling it with ice and letting it sit while you prepare the drink. This will help keep your cocktail cold.

Mix the ingredients: In a mixing glass, combine the aquavit, dry vermouth, Pernod or absinthe, and two dashes of orange bitters.

Add ice: Fill the mixing glass with ice. Stir the mixture well for about 30 seconds to properly chill and dilute the drink.

Strain into the glass: Empty the ice from the chilled cocktail glass. Strain the mixture from the mixing glass into the chilled cocktail glass.

Garnish with a cucumber slice.

And yes… if you want the cucumber to be slightly bruised, just tap it on the countertop two times.

# You're Dedicated… But Are You Kamikaze Dedicated?

Back in 2020, I met a guy named Oscar who had an interesting personality. He worked nonstop and hustled 24/7. Now, I've met these types of people many times throughout my life. It's nothing new. However, it was the first time I met someone who not only hustled like this, but conversed about it constantly… and I'm not talking about working nonstop or about his work specifically, but rather bragging about his grind skills and the hustle lifestyle.

"I don't hang with anyone that isn't crushing it… I won't even waste a second talking to those types of folks. I only have time to talk with winners. Your network is your net worth."

I quickly learned that this is a trend called hustle culture. It's where folks believe the most important characteristic of life is to not only achieve serious professional goals by relentlessly working like a corporate raider, but also to talk about it until they're the most insufferable prick in the room. For these folks, any hope of self-fulfillment revolves around the grind and the personal sacrifice.

I call it someone who never gets laid… and if he did, he'd probably let the woman know his favorite position is CEO.

Or he'd say some other equally douchey thing.

For Oscar, I had to deal with him for several years because he was part of a circle that included a few of my business acquaintances. While many of these folks had some small degree of this personality type in them, myself included, this guy was absurd. One day, it just went too far.

We were at a social club discussing some business. I was interested in partnering with a particular businessman to open a bar. I'd always wanted to own a cool little pub, had a great idea for a concept, and thought one of the guys there, Jimmy, would make a great associate for the venture.

Jimmy loved the idea and mentioned that he knew one of the most successful people in town, Denny Macklin, who owned several bars and clubs. Jimmy suggested we get some advice from him about my concept.

"His dad owned those bars and clubs. Denny inherited all that," Oscar said.

"Okay, so what?" I replied. "Denny has been running them successfully for over 15 years, even expanded well beyond what his father started."

"All I'm saying is this, Sean: You're not grinding hard enough if your dad owns the company. I wouldn't be okay with any of that silver spoon shit."

What a weird flex. Are you saying you would rather be born to poor, struggling parents? Who the fuck would choose that over rich, successful parents?

My sarcastic side surfaced.

"Oscar, you're clearly dedicated, and I respect that, but are you Kamikaze dedicated? You're not. We're not the same."

The group chuckled.

"You wanna mock and hate on me? Cool, bro, just remember this: The more haters like you hate, the harder I grind until the day you, and the rest of the haters, ask me for a job."

I would rather run backwards through a field of dicks than ever work for you.

While this personality is basically that of an alpha male, it also has another cousin known as sigma males. Sigma males, seemingly a relatively new term, are males who exhibit the same kind of alpha traits but aren't boisterous or particularly social… like alpha males for introverts.

With hustle culture, these folks basically relate to sigma males only in the way that 24/7 hustle keeps you out of social circles and leaves no time for women. Women may say they're just using that as a cover for their own inability to handle real relationships. They're not men… they're just boys who can't deal with real women.

Let me explain something to you, honey. Men chase women… legends chase money. You are not part of their mindset, because that interferes with their grindset.

For Oscar, and most everyone else who does this, it's probably more of a personal motivation tool than it is a serious way to live, but that doesn't seem worth it. It's funny and entertaining for me, but probably a personal nightmare for them. Can you imagine living this way? This cannot be fun, and the stress has to be brutal… plus, you're not getting laid or even finding enough time to pound a few drinks and relax for an hour or two.

I said all of that to Oscar.

He took it personally.

"Bro, you're mad because I'm the rock that turns into a diamond under that pressure. You're the rock that turns to dust."

"Oscar, you're a pescatarian because you're a health freak. I'm a vegetarian because I fucking hate plants. We're not the same."

The group chuckled.

Look, at the end of the day, you're free to be whomever you want. Just because I find you to be a big asshat who continually comes off as an overbearing and irritating schmuck, that doesn't mean you are… it's just what I think you are.

No, I take it back… you *are* exactly that.

You can tell me you have my best interest in mind, that working 365 days a year is not toxic, that it's a map for success I should be following. You can say that anyone who tells me different is someone who just wants to hold me back… and I will let you know you're wrong.

You need to work 366 days, because it's a leap year, ya bitch!

# The 30-Minutes-or-it's-Free Pizza Delivery Guys From the 1980s are the True Heroes

I ordered a pizza the other night and was disappointed. Not with the pizza, but with the delivery driver… and not in the way you think. The service was fine. He, on the other hand, was a sad man.

What happened to these folks?

As I took the pie from his hands, he looked at me with his cold, dead eyes and didn't even flinch, even after I gave him a sizable tip. He just took a picture of the pizza, pocketed the tip, set his GPS to the next address, and drifted off slowly back toward his car, staring into his phone.

Back when I was a kid, these guys were the most badass people and some of the toughest folks. They were risking their lives, as well as the lives of others, to get pizza to you in under 30 minutes… even your shitty pineapple-topped pizza.

They didn't judge. They just delivered in under 30 minutes or less, or it was free.

And they did this without smartphones, GPS, sunlight, or Siri telling them to make a left turn… nothing but a shitty 1970 Toyota Corolla and balls of steel.

Let's do the math: How long does it take to actually make a pizza and get that bitch out on the road? At least 10 minutes…

probably more like 15, depending on how stoned the employee was when he or she started making the pie.

That leaves 15 minutes to get to your door or it's free. Well, free for you. The driver who gives out too many free pizzas would likely be out of a job in 30 minutes or less. And it wasn't just the clock, traffic, and the lack of technology slowing them down. Keep in mind that a lot of customers were total dicks, doing everything they could to delay delivery or throw the driver off.

Turning off porch lights was common. That was effective occasionally, albeit some basic-ass rookie shit. There were customers purposely blocking addresses, either by pulling the light bulbs out of their illuminated address plaques or putting trash cans in front of addresses painted on curbs. Nice try, bitches, but drivers in the 1980s carried mag flashlights. Shit looked like a police helicopter canvassing the neighborhood for the assholes who pulled these types of bullshit moves. Some ass-wipes would take it to the next level by draping street signs with towels or blankets in their neighborhood so delivery drivers didn't know what street they were on or where to turn.

Any way they could fuck over a delivery driver for a free pizza.

And if there was a problem that needed immediate attention, there were no cell phones, so drivers had to know where every gas station or convenience store was with a pay phone… and they still could pull deliveries off in time.

Some drivers just reinvented the delivery game altogether, such as using scooters and mopeds to drive down alleyways, backroads, and sidewalks. They would cut through parks, parking lots, and even go the wrong way down one-way streets, swerving through oncoming traffic, and a host of other shortcuts that cars couldn't pull off. The more customers tried to fuck the drivers for a free pizza, the more the drivers fucked the customers out of a free pizza.

Today's delivery drivers couldn't hold these guys' pizza delivery bags. Delivery drivers today have NASA-level technology: satellites, artificial intelligence guiding them to the shortest routes, GPS systems barking out every traffic situation in real time, apps that basically make it impossible to fuck a delivery up… and even self-driving cars.

They're pathetic.

Last week I attended a gala for educators in Los Angeles. As I listened to each speaker, I was fascinated by how often the word "hero" was used to describe teachers and others in the field. That got me thinking about how often that word is overused, especially today. Don't get me wrong, I believe that educators are selfless and inspirational folks who serve the community's most important people: The kids.

But heroes?

How many of us have delivered a pizza in under 30 minutes during the dark ages before the Internet?

# Smoke Detectors Can Save Your Life...
# I'd Rather Die.

Last year my wife and I started looking for our dream house... well, her dream house. You know how that goes. We found a beautiful two-story home that was upgraded and modernized with some of the most beautiful kitchen, living room, and bathroom setups I had ever seen... even the guest bathroom had one of those high-end walk-in, all-glass showers. The master bedroom had a balcony overlooking a pool and Jacuzzi, with a bathroom that had a shower fit for kings and a jet tub that could fit a small army.

I was all in. This place was perfect... except for one thing I noticed when we were leaving. On the ceiling that stretched high above the den, there was a smoke alarm.

Fuck this house. That ceiling had to be 30 feet above my head. Eventually that smoke alarm's battery will drain and begin beeping... and it will do it at 3 a.m., because, for some reason, smoke alarm low-battery signals only go off between the hours of 11 p.m. and 4 a.m., guaranteed, every time.

My wife blasted me for overreacting.

"So, we'll just take it down and replace it, putting the new one someplace more accessible."

I looked at the real estate agent.

"Is that hardwired into the house?"

"Yes," she said.

I looked at my wife.

"Yeah, fuck that. I'm not buying this place."

There is a universal law of the universe, right up there with gravity and lost socks: the smoke detector low-battery chirp will only begin at 2:00 a.m. Never 3:00 p.m., when you're alert and have the energy of a fully functioning adult. No, it waits until you're deep in REM sleep, dreaming of a world where household appliances don't conspire against you.

Let's talk about that battery compartment. You'd think a device designed to save lives would have a user-friendly system for changing its power source. But no. Instead, the battery hatch is secured like it's guarding nuclear launch codes. And do you have a screwdriver handy at 2 a.m.? Of course not. You have a shoe, which you will absolutely use in a futile attempt to pry it open before giving up and just yanking the whole thing off the ceiling.

And thus, the cycle begins again… because that fresh battery will eventually die… and when it does, it will again be at 2 a.m. When will this happen? That's part of the fun. It could be in a few months, maybe a year, maybe a few years. Nevertheless, it will happen in the dead of night.

Before you start ripping me apart about how many lives these devices have saved and how a little inconvenience is a small price to pay, I understand that. Smoke detectors have been crucial in home fire safety since their invention in the 1930s. Early models were expensive and primarily used in industrial settings. However, in 1965, Duane Pearsall and Stanley Bennett Peterson developed the first affordable battery-operated smoke detector, making home use practical. By the 1970s, smoke detectors became widely available, leading to increased adoption and legal requirements.

In the U.S., smoke detector regulations vary by state and local jurisdictions, but key national standards exist. The National Fire Protection Association (NFPA) provides guidelines, and the U.S. Consumer Product Safety Commission promotes safety regulations. The 1976 passage of the Federal Fire Prevention and Control Act required smoke alarms in new homes, and many states later mandated them in existing residences.

Modern laws require smoke detectors in bedrooms, hallways, and each floor of a home. Many states mandate hardwired alarms with battery backups, and newer regulations require sealed, 10-year lithium battery models to reduce maintenance issues. Landlords must ensure smoke detectors are functional, and homeowners are advised to test them monthly. As technology advances, smart smoke detectors with connectivity features are becoming more common, further enhancing fire safety in homes worldwide.

You would think all of these improvements would make these devices easier to deal with, but they don't… the irony is that the more they improve and modernize these devices, the more of a pain in the ass they become. In the old days, I just had to take these down, crack them open, remove the battery, and then go back to bed. That was a pain in the ass, but at least it was doable. Now, with all these "modern advances," I have to find the correct twist pattern to line up the release points so I can remove it from the ceiling. Then I have to disconnect the hard wiring to take it fully down, then find the kill switch to disable it since they all have internal batteries. Keep in mind, that kill switch is permanent. At least in the old days, I just had to replace the battery… now I have to take a trip to Home Depot and replace the entire unit. Built-in obsolescence is great for business, not for my pocketbook or my sanity. That kill switch is designed to be difficult to flip so you don't accidentally do it to a brand-new unit and ruin it.

For the record, I'm coming at this problem from experience. I lived in a huge house years ago with a bunch of roommates during college that had this issue. This was one of those McMansions… six bedrooms, about 3,000 square feet, and ceilings that touched the heavens. I lived in the master bedroom on the main floor. My ceilings were about 15 feet high, with a smoke alarm that would be hard to reach even if I were LeBron James.

The problem started one night randomly, at 3 a.m., of course, because that's when these devices decide to either signal their low battery or, worse, become possessed by some mischievous fire safety demon bent on ruining my night. It started with a single, ear-splitting BEEP. I shot out of bed, convinced the house was ablaze. After a frantic, pants-less investigation, I discovered there was no fire, just the cursed alarm screaming false prophecies of doom. I went to the garage and got a ladder and a broomstick so I could reach the alarm and push the button to silence it. I tried to go back to sleep, but just as I drifted off… BEEP BEEP BEEP.

This battle raged for days as I waited patiently for the landlord to fix the problem… he didn't. I decided my only course of action was to cut the breaker to the alarm system, which in turn also killed a number of outlets. We had to run an extension cord for the fridge to another working outlet. Only God knows what happened after I moved out. Some say it still haunts that ceiling.

When I bought my first house in the summer of 2007, I had wired-in smoke detectors and never had a problem. Then, as winter approached, one night, a smoke detector in a guest bedroom went off… you want to guess what time? Of course you know the answer to this. Again, I jumped out of my bed thinking my new house was turning into a match, only to find that there was nothing. I simply pushed the button and went back to bed. Well, 30 minutes later, it went off again. This time I just pulled it down. I replaced the unit, assuming it was defective, but the new unit went off. You want to know what time that was? No curveball being thrown this time. It was 1 a.m. I had a guy come out and check the wired system, and everything was fine… there was no reason for this. However, for the next few days, I dealt with this until I just removed the alarm completely. My girlfriend at the time didn't like this… it wasn't safe.

After months of nagging and her convincing me that the new alarm I bought must have been defective, I bought a new one and installed it. By this time, spring had rolled around. Why is that important? Keep reading. It's important. We had no problems, and I conceded to her that she was right. The old detector was faulty, and the one I bought to replace it was equally faulty. The odds of this? Not likely, but that was the only explanation. Spring through summer, there were zero issues. Then, when winter arrived, suddenly, at 3 a.m., of course, the alarm went off.

It was a hair-pulling level of frustration. What the fuck was going on? I pulled the alarm down, vowing to never replace it. It was only weeks later that a conversation with a contractor finally solved the mystery.

"How close is the alarm to your ceiling vent?" he asked.

"Right next to it."

"That's your issue... the heat coming out of the vent is setting it off. It's why it only goes off in the winter. Whoever installed these alarms screwed up."

The cost to move the alarm and reroute the wiring was more than I was willing to part with. Fuck that alarm. I'd rather die in the fire.

Now, I know what you're thinking... losing one alarm in your house can increase the likelihood that I won't catch a fire early enough if it starts in that area. There is some risk. However, if there were an actual fire, are you even sure you would actually know that?

Can you tell me what the beeps are? I learned this from the carbon monoxide detectors. The device starts going off. Was it a fire? Low battery? Carbon monoxide? Wiring issue? End-of-life warning... yes... if you haven't found this out yet, you will. Detectors now have a built-in lifespan. They will begin a series of beeps to let you know to replace it.

I had a detector go off in a way I had never heard... however, despite this new and unfamiliar pattern of beeps, two things still stayed the same: It was loud as fuck and went off at 2 a.m. I consulted the manual, which was just a cryptic list of beep patterns:

- One beep every 30 seconds – Low battery

- Two beeps every minute – Needs replacing

- Three beeps, pause, three beeps – Fire detected

- Four beeps, pause, four beeps – Carbon monoxide

- Five beeps – Get the fuck up and quit asking questions.

After twenty minutes of detective work, I gave up and pulled the unit down... again. I sighed. I'd just have to live knowing that if a fire ever happened, I'd probably ignore it.

# Your Will: Leave Enough So They're Grateful, But Not Enough to Want to Kill You

I grew up in a family of lawyers. My mom was a lawyer, and so were two of my uncles. I learned a lot about the law and it's some of the most valuable information I could have ever gained. Most folks do not grasp their rights when they face any legal issues, nor do they fully understand when they have a potential lawsuit. It's really daunting, and I'm glad I was privileged enough to be taught the deeper ins and outs of the law, my rights, and how to best approach any legal situation.

However, out of all the things I learned, the most important legal information wasn't how to handle cops when you get arrested or what you're legally required to do when they haul you off to jail. It wasn't how to handle a bad divorce or how to best work around taxes or create shelters. It wasn't even learning about the detailed legal protection I have in my place of employment. None of these even came close to the most important thing I learned.

When you draft a will, make sure folks get enough to be grateful but not so much that they want to kill you to collect the inheritance.

Don't be foolish. It happens more than you think… and we all know the justice system is not fair nor concrete. It has a lot of variables. For example, if a woman terminates a pregnancy, it's a choice, but if I drive my car into a playground full of children, it's murder.

You see what I'm saying?

My point is this: People are willing to take their chances murdering someone, even if they know they are likely going to be a main suspect, because we see folks who clearly are guilty get away with it a lot of times. Do you really want to give anyone a good reason to play the odds?

I know what you're thinking. Murdering someone for the inheritance is rare and really not a concern one should worry about. You may be right. While experts will admit there are some instances of people killing to acquire an inheritance, they also claim that it's extremely uncommon compared to the overall number of legal issues involving inheritance cases. However, there is no specific database or comprehensive source that tracks the number of people killed over a will, be it to get the money or in a dispute over the money after a death. The experts claim that inheritance-related murders are often sensationalized in media and in popular culture, but statistically, they are extremely rare. When such cases do arise, they typically involve an overwhelming level of greed and/or other complex factors such as financial desperation or pre-existing conflicts within families. It's not as simple as someone who is greedy deciding to kill a family member. There are a number of factors in play and usually a long history of issues. No one who has a great relationship with someone for decades suddenly decides to kill them after they find out they're in a will.

This makes total sense, but I'm still skeptical. Statistics are like bikinis: what they reveal is suggestive, but what they conceal is vital. Fact of the matter is this type of shit happens all the time, even if it is rare. Remember, "where there's a will, there's a way" is a great self-motivational phrase until an inheritance is involved.

Consider the case of Nathan Carmen, a Vermont man who was arrested and charged with killing his mother to inherit her fortune of over $7 million in 2023. Did he do it? Most likely he did, but we'll never really know. Nathan killed himself while awaiting trial. Some applauded this, saying that the suicide saved taxpayers money on a trial for a man that most believe brutally killed his mom. I don't agree with that rationale. We needed a trial to make sure we found the total truth.

However, I get why people were happy with how it ended. I just don't think that's the best outcome. Hey, I used to think that suicide would solve all my problems too, but the issue was getting the people that were causing my problems to go through with it.

Or wait… maybe he didn't kill himself. Who was in his will? There was still $7 million in the tank.

We're on a tangent here. Let's refocus. The question is this: How much do you leave someone? Determining how much to leave someone in a will depends on various factors, including your relationship with the person, your assets, their needs, and your wishes. Here are some considerations to keep in mind.

Let's start with your relationship to the individual. Are they a spouse, child, sibling, friend, or another very close relative? Closer relationships might warrant a larger portion of your estate, but that also generally means you're closer in proximity, which can be a huge problem. My Uncle Bob isn't that close to me, but that's also because he doesn't live close to me. He lives down south. You can't slowly poison my breakfast every day from Alabama… plus, where I live, murder is much harder to pull off. You can kill someone in Alabama and get away with it since there are no dental records, and most DNA samples lead back to every single person in town.

Bottom line: You're not near me, so it's harder to get to me.

Next, assess the financial needs of the beneficiary. If they have specific financial obligations or challenges, you may want to allocate more to support them. Or, if they have been an absolute dick, leave them all the shit you would have had to pay a company to pick up and dump. You save time and money for the relatives you do like and make the pricks you don't like have to clean out your house… and they'll be cleaning out your house while having to act like they're grateful for the 500 worthless Hummel figurines you left them.

Finally, let's look at all the other beneficiaries we haven't covered. You'll need to balance the needs and desires of different individuals, regardless of relationship. Generally, though, you don't want to leave the outlying folks much of anything, if anything at all, because it may not take too much for these folks to end your life for the inheritance. I don't mean in a murder plot or anything that dramatic, but more like not helping you when you need it. For example, if you were choking on some food at dinner, this guy wouldn't jump up to administer the Heimlich maneuver, just fake panic as you squirm on the floor, touching the hand of God because you didn't masticate a piece of steak long enough. So, that dude will never actually kill you but will take advantage of any situation where you nominate yourself for a Darwin Award.

Then you have to consider the legal and tax implications of any assets you leave behind. Now, this varies from state to state, but do keep in mind that the government will always try to get their cut. Death and taxes: The two things you cannot avoid. On the bright side, at least Congress doesn't meet every two years to make death worse, so there's that. Consult with a financial lawyer to understand any legal or tax implications of your decisions, as well as to find out how to legally fuck the government out of grave-robbing you.

For some, I know they will roll their eyes when you tell them to hire a lawyer. As the old saying goes: If you have a gun with only two bullets and you're stuck in a room with a serial killer, a bomb-strapped terrorist, and a lawyer, who do you shoot? You shoot the lawyer… twice… and if you planned this correctly, that lawyer will have left you a fat inheritance.

# Real-World Skills Should Be Taught in School, but Kids Still Won't Give a Fuck

Throughout my teaching career, I often heard students say this: "When will I use Shakespeare in the real world?" Math teachers get the same types of questions: "When am I ever going to use calculus?" We've all heard these comments, and most of us probably asked our own teachers the same questions when we were in school. It's an old cliché.

However, in the last decade, this question, uttered by multiple generations, has found a new life of its own on social media with young adults who are struggling to adjust to the real world. No longer is the question just being sarcastically asked by kids in high school; rather, it's now a talking point for Generation Z as the foundation for why they cannot handle basic functions of being an adult. This includes things such as taxes, loans, personal finance, wealth building, etc. According to these young folks, it's the schools' fault for not teaching them the skills they needed to know, but instead wasted their time teaching them things that never applied.

There are memes, comments, and posts all over social media about this. Yet, with all the complaining about what high school did not teach them, most of these memes and comments happen to omit one little caveat about teaching these real-life skills...

something that would render their claims about what they weren't taught a bit shaky.

Be it Shakespeare or taxes, it wouldn't matter... most high school students don't give a fuck. How do I know this? I taught these very things in my high school classes many times... or at least tried to do it.

Most folks on the campus where I worked knew that I had amassed quite a nest egg investing, including many of the students. I never hid this fact or shied away from it, as I openly talked about the stock market and real estate and my involvement in both for decades. One day in class, the students blew off my lesson on database research strategies. If the students weren't talking to their friends as if I wasn't there, they were on their phones or sleeping. I got frustrated and asked them what they wanted to do since my lesson wasn't important to them. They asked why I did not teach them real-world things that matter. So I asked this question: "What do you want to know? How I made my fortune? I could teach you how to do that."

Suddenly, conversations stopped and they put down their phones.

"I'm interested," the collective group said. "This is what we should be learning."

I began by explaining where I started with stocks, mainly because it has a low barrier of entry and doesn't require a lot of money to get into the game. I told them investing can be complex, but it doesn't have to be and, in fact, is quite easy to understand once you get some basics down. I told them I used a long-term dividend strategy and parlayed that into real estate with minimum amounts of money down, explaining that after you purchase your first property, you can leverage that property's value and equity into expanding and growing your assets into millions. It doesn't happen overnight, but it will happen as long as you do not take unnecessary risks.

For the record, I actually didn't say all of this… I didn't get past the first two sentences. By the time I picked up the whiteboard marker, almost every kid just went back to their phone.

It's a boring and dry subject… and most high school students don't give a fuck about this type of shit. It's surprising, really. This was about personal finance, one of the things Generation Z seems to be most upset about adults not teaching them years earlier. It's also about getting wealthy, something teenagers are all about. Isn't this what today's young adults say they wanted to learn?

Congratulations, Gen Z… your superpower is hindsight. You're the Aquaman of adulting.

This is the gaslighting that many young folks do today. They're unclear about these things, it can impact their life in a negative way, it's difficult to understand, or it takes effort to work through and learn… and then they blame the teachers and schools for not teaching them these vital life skills, acting as if they wouldn't have been so dismissive of public education if they were taught real-world lessons instead of useless stuff like Shakespeare. According to Gen Z, it wasn't them, but rather the curriculum schools picked. If they were taught real-world stuff back in high school, they would have been totally engaged.

I taught for 20 years, and can tell you this: Most high school students don't give a fuck.

Taxes are a big one that young adults complain about not being taught. When that was brought up in my classes, I told students it was easy to do and that if they wanted me to teach them the fundamentals, I would. Of course they said yes. I pulled up a 1040 form and started to explain how taxes worked at a basic level, in terms of giving the government some of the money you make throughout the year, then calculating what you actually owe at the end of the year. If you paid them too much, you get money back. If you paid too little, you owe the difference. I explained that this is the type of filing most folks will do on their own, but then informed them that if one expands beyond a basic job, starts amassing investments, gets married and has kids, buys a house, or goes into business for themselves, they would most likely hire a tax person to handle it. This is where I started talking about write-offs and tax breaks.

By the way, most every student just went back to their phone once I uttered the first sentence and pulled up a 1040 form on my wall projector.

Most students… they don't give a fuck about this shit.

Gen Z also complains about how they were never taught the fundamentals about debt or how loans and interest work. I taught this to seniors… or at least I tried. I pulled up an amortization calculator and began to explain how banks make money by loaning it out and was going to show them how student loans, buying a car, and buying a house work in terms of interest rates.

What do you think happened? I'll give you a hint: They didn't give a fuck.

Then there's the shit they bitch about that makes no sense… we should teach them car maintenance. What the fuck? If they took the time and effort to learn about all the other shit on this list, they would likely end up successful enough to afford a mechanic. In fact, with the way cars are built today, unless you have an automotive repair education and thousands of dollars in specialized tools, you're not fixing shit. The only reason a person would attempt to work on their own car in this day and age is because they have no choice. Why don't you perform your own dentistry too while you're at it?

Here's the sad part about all of this: Most of this stuff is taught in school as part of economics class, which is required senior year. So, it's not that the school never taught it, because they did… the kids blew it off. You may ask yourself: "Why would they do this? This is information they could use in the real world."

Well, the answer is quite simple: They don't give a fuck.

# A Conversation with a Spirit is Not Credible Evidence

For the record, I was not absent from work for 40 days. I was just present somewhere else.

Ah yes… the "my truth" movement. The newest incarnation of reality has finally arrived. No longer just twisting narratives or spinning facts to make things look a bit different, but rather creating one's own version of them. It seems now one's own thoughts, beliefs, and opinions are facts, no matter how absurd they are… even if you can prove the person to be 100 percent wrong.

If that's the case, to all the women I have disappointed sexually in my life, I want to say it wasn't disappointment as much as it was frustration with my intensity. It's a lot to handle, and being the best lover you ever had, I know it can create those feelings of frustration.

It's okay; I forgive you. You're welcome.

However, we have to draw the line somewhere, and I think I may have found that line.

If we're in a disagreement or a debate about a topic, you cannot use a conversation you had with a dead person using a Ouija board as evidence. I'm going to need to see actual proof that you talked with a dead person.

"Oh, I talked to a spirit, period."

Now, for the record, it's a known fact that in the *my truth* movement, if you say the word "period" at the end of a statement, what you just said is the stone-cold truth, period.

See what I did there?

Still, I'm not accepting this.

This isn't *The Sixth Sense* and you're not Truth Willis.

Normally, I wouldn't care. If you want to believe in the existence of tiny fairy-like creatures that guard treasure or the power of tiki totems, that's fine. We're just never going to agree this bullshit is real or that these things have magical powers… and you can't use the fact that your house hasn't been robbed ever since you put gnomes or totems in your yard as evidence that these powers work. My ball sack keeps tigers away. Don't believe me? Do you see any tigers around my junk? Exactly.

This is just belief perseverance and denialism. Yes, these are two real theories in psychology. Belief perseverance is believing something even more after it's been debunked, and denialism is when a person chooses to deny reality as a way to avoid a psychologically uncomfortable truth… and who would want my balls or a tiger in their front yard? I would avoid that uncomfortable truth too.

I really thought the flat Earth movement from a decade ago was the pinnacle of denying facts, but here we are a decade later… and telling me that you'll walk to the ends of the Earth to prove your point still doesn't make the Earth flat. It's the same with the conspiracy that Abraham Lincoln was never assassinated and John Wilkes Booth was a fabricated person. The Earth is round, and Lincoln was killed by that madman.

That's the John Wilkes Truth, period.

You can't get any dumber than this, right? Wanna bet?

There is a whole movement of folks that believe in urine therapy. According to these fuckwits, there is nothing that urine won't cure. Everything from the common cold to cancer, they believe that it all can be eradicated with piss. Sometimes they ingest it, or they'll spread it all over their bodies. Sometimes cold... sometimes straight from the source.

I guess this officially makes at least one category on Pornhub a health and wellness channel.

This isn't new, and the idea has been around for centuries, but the practice slowed down when this thing called science came out and let us know that pissing ourselves doesn't really help anything. Despite all science debunking any benefits of urine, people still argue about this. An Indian company actually tried to market a drink containing cow urine back in 2009 as a move to promote wellbeing, claiming the product replenished one's health and energy.

Don't worry, Gatorade, I think you're still safe.

If you slow down a VHS tape that was recorded 30 years ago, you can see that former President Bill Clinton is a lizard. I also can watch a Charlie Chaplin movie from the 1930s and see more lines than I would see on Charlie Sheen's coffee table. Maybe it's just an old tape. Did you ever consider that?

We've arrived… the lizard people conspiracy theorists. These folks believe most high-ranking government officials, world leaders, and the rich are actually reptilians disguised as humans trying to… well… I guess take over the world? I don't know what they think, but it's more than 4% of registered voters that believe this garbage. That's more than five million people total. Hold up… if these lizard people are currently all the world's most influential, richest, and powerful people, then why are the believers saying that they're *trying* to take over the world? They already have control of everything and the money. It's not like all these lizard people are cab drivers, Denny's servers, and dental hygienists. If that was the case, and you said they're here to take over the world, then it makes sense.

Wait… no it doesn't. None of this shit makes any sense. Why the fuck am I trying to figure this out? The lizard people aren't real. It's the plot of that miniseries *V* from the 1980s. Maybe we should all pray that lizard people are real, they're here, and taking over. I mean, I wouldn't put much faith in our new reptilian overlords, but at this point, I may have more faith in them than I do the actual human race.

# I Wrote About O.J. Simpson, but I Think it's Too Tasteless

I rarely find myself in a position of self-debate about what I write and whether or not it crosses a line. Two reasons for this: One, I do not go out of my way to write outwardly offensive stuff. I'm not trying to be a provocateur. Two, I think comedy and satire are designed to push limits beyond boundaries, and sometimes that makes people uncomfortable or upsets them. Essentially, I support any humor at any time, even if it may cross lines in some folks' eyes.

However, this piece I wrote about O.J. Simpson... I don't know... maybe it's a bit "too much." I'm on the fence. I think it's funny, but I also came up with the idea and wrote it. I'm biased. On the other hand, part of me also recognizes that not everyone will get the humor... or even if they get the humor, they still may not find it funny or acceptable.

The real issue I'm struggling with is I have this piece I spent time on, that I think is a funny concept/idea, that challenged me as a writer in a few ways, and now I feel I have to shelve it for these reasons. What do I do? Maybe I should write about the article? At minimum, the concept/idea won't be wasted, and this will be cathartic for me as I deal with this dilemma.

First, let me give credit where credit is due. The idea for this piece came from two separate inspirations: an old Norm Macdonald joke about Simpson and several recent articles discussing how Simpson's legacy will not be about his football greatness, the 1973 record-breaking season, nor his massive mainstream appeal, but rather the murders and nothing else.

Let's start with the Norm Macdonald joke.

O.J. Simpson's lawyers have decided to skip hearings on DNA evidence and go right to trial. Asked why they did this, the lawyers replied, "We want to get O.J. acquitted as speedily as possible, so he can get back to doing what he does best: killing people."

This old joke resurfaced in my head as I read numerous articles discussing his legacy. Suddenly, the idea bloomed: O.J. Simpson was arguably the greatest running back the NFL had ever seen. His 1973 rushing record will likely never be broken. However, he won't be remembered for any of that. He'll be remembered for the murders, and that's it. Well, is he the best running back ever? Norm said murdering is what he does best. I thought to myself… could I mold these two things together? Basically, what if I wrote a story that seemingly leaned toward discussing his legacy being about that 1973 record and his storied career, but then kept switching to the record O.J. has that no other athlete will ever break: his ability to knife two people to death in under ten minutes and get away with it, even though he was clearly guilty.

Read on… this will make more sense in a minute.

Here's the approach I was crafting. I decided to take the voice of a sportswriter, where I would describe all of these skills that O.J. possessed, which are the reasons why he ran for a mind-bending 143 yards-per-game average in 1973 and why he had such a dominant career. I attempted a narrative that sounded like a sports analyst's breakdown of Simpson's skills and why they were so effective on the field… then, each time I would do this, I would jump into explaining in the same voice and style how these skills also made him an unmatched, effective double-murderer.

Then I compare Simpson to other disgraced football players and how they cannot match O.J. on the field nor off the field, like it's a debate about who is the GOAT of murderous athletes. Again, this is all in the same voice as if I'm talking about who the greatest quarterback of all time is and trying to explain why or support my position.

So, if you haven't figured out why this may be "too much," let me clarify. The issue is I talk about Simpson's exceptional skills on the field and why these skills made him so great. I then go on to discuss how these same skills applied when he killed two people, making him the GOAT of murderous athletes. Here's an example of what it reads like:

"No other running back in the history of the game has ever matched the combination of swiftness, strength, and the unique pairing of both the authority he ran with and the dexterity he displayed. Simpson was a fusion of physical might and rapid artfulness, allowing him to break tackles and evade defenders with relative ease. Still, his 1973 season cannot match the combination of speed, power, and agility he displayed on June 12, 1994…"

Imagine where it goes next. Apply the same voice/style and the things I say about him on the field to the murders. It's funny to me, but as I said earlier, I'm biased and not easily offended, if I can even be offended. Others may feel different and, frankly, I wouldn't blame them. I'm self-aware enough to know exactly what I wrote and empathetic enough not to run with something just because "I think it's funny" or "creative."

I'm also very aware of the fact that even if folks understand what I'm attempting to do, that doesn't mean it's not in poor taste. When I read the final draft, even I said, "Man, this is really pushing it." Do I think this is in poor taste? Personally, in my eyes, no… I don't think it is, but I also have a different philosophy about creative ventures than others. In my opinion, nothing can truly be in "poor taste" because everyone's opinions on that vary. I see art in a way that others likely do not, so my conclusions will be different. However, that doesn't mean I cannot recognize why something is seen by others to be in poor taste. The difference with me is I may still find it funny regardless of what anyone says, or even if I find it in poor taste as well. I still think it's a creative piece and funny. I'm just very aware that others may not see it this way at all. For now it will sit until I figure out what to do with it.

# On Second Thought, Fuck O.J. Simpson

Looking back, I'm surprised I even thought writing about O.J. Simpson could ever be too tasteless. However, I do understand that there are victims here, and my reluctance was really about them. I get the conundrum, but let's just say what everyone's been dancing around for decades like it's a polite cocktail party and not the aftermath of a double homicide: Fuck O.J. Simpson. He murdered people... allegedly... but also, come on.

I'm publishing my article, and I have more reasons to do it versus not doing it.

In the grand American tradition of rewarding fame over basic morality, O.J. Simpson managed to ride through the fire of brutally murdering Nicole Brown Simpson and Ron Goldman and came out the other end relatively unscathed. Of course he was ostracized by many, but not by all. He didn't just walk free. He strutted with golf clubs in hand, grinning like he'd just dodged a parking ticket, not a life sentence. Then came the book *If I Did It,* which might as well have been titled *Of Course I Did It, But Try Proving It.* Who else writes a hypothetical confession unless they're either a sociopath or auditioning for the world's darkest improv show? They even attempted to give this maniac his own reality prank show titled *Juiced,* which lasted one episode. O.J. dressing up in costume and pranking unsuspecting folks has to be near the top of the most sadistic things you could greenlight in Hollywood, especially since one prank involved stabbing. It was bad enough when Ashton Kutcher did it, but when they revealed the prank at the height of the emotional rollercoaster the mark was on, it was a lovable and jovial Ashton coming out to bring them down and reveal that it all was a joke… not a guy that killed two people.

O.J. also gave us The Kardashians, gave careers to hack legal analysts, made wearing certain gloves unacceptable, and, probably worst of all, gave Americans the gift of becoming so desensitized they now think "alleged double murderer" is just part of a quirky backstory. Sure, let's keep pretending he's just a misunderstood football legend who occasionally stabs people in hypotheticals. In a perfect world, O.J. would've been remembered for breaking tackles, not decapitating women. But that isn't reality. He killed two people and, unfortunately, we live in a nation where you can beat the system if you're famous, your smile is charming, you're rich, and your lawyer can rhyme.

So, yeah, fuck O.J. Simpson. He murdered folks… and the only thing that was more absurd than his freedom was the fact that when he was still here he had some semblance of a social life and social media accounts where he could go live and act like his murder trial was just a minor bump in the road of an otherwise scandal-free life.

# O.J. Simpson's Legacy Will Be for a Record No Athlete Will Ever Break: Double Murder in Minutes and Acquittal

When O.J. Simpson passed away in 2024 it was the end of a long and complicated era. Still remembered as one of the greatest running backs to ever play in the National Football League, his record-breaking 1973 season, where he averaged 143.1 yards a game, has never been matched… and probably never will. However, his greatest record is even more astonishing, with no other athlete able to even come close to it.

In cold blood, he knifed two people to death in under ten minutes and got away with it, even though he was clearly guilty.

Athletes from across every sport have done some fucked-up shit, including murder. However, none have even come close to matching O.J.'s savagery and cunningness with a double homicide while managing to simultaneously avoid prison, despite the fact that every piece of evidence pointed directly to him as the perpetrator.

This is a feat that is simply untouchable.

First, just a quick recap: Nicole Brown Simpson, O.J. Simpson's ex-wife, and her friend Ronald Goldman were found murdered outside Nicole's condominium in the Brentwood area of Los Angeles in June of 1994. Both victims had been stabbed multiple times. The Los Angeles Police Department described it as one of the most brutal attacks they had ever seen. Keep in mind, this is Los Angeles we're talking about… home to the crimes of Charles Manson and the Night Stalker Richard Ramirez.

Prior to this, O.J. Simpson had already done things on the field that no other athlete could, or ever will, come close to accomplishing. In 1973, when he had arguably the best season a running back has ever had, he displayed a superhuman-like talent. That record-breaking year has never been duplicated by anyone else. This defined most of his playing career. No other running back in the history of the game has ever matched the combination of swiftness, strength, and the unique pairing of both the authority he ran with and the dexterity he displayed. Simpson was a fusion of physical might and rapid artfulness, allowing him to break tackles and evade defenders with relative ease.

Still, his 1973 season cannot match the combination of speed, power, and agility he displayed on June 12, 1994. First, he showed up to Nicole's place only expecting to deal with his ex-wife, but quickly managed to change his game plan with the unexpected arrival of another individual. Even with another person entering the scene, he could immediately adjust and kill them too with ruthless efficiency. Simpson displayed his peerless combination of fluid movements with an impressive ability to accelerate quickly and change direction rapidly. Whether it was in his 20s or in his 40s, Simpson had a unique blend of strength and finesse, allowing him to either bulldoze defenders down or juke them without ever being touched, be it a linebacker on the field or two innocent victims fighting for their lives.

None of this is surprising at all. His running style involved a low center of gravity, allowing him to maintain balance while navigating through defenders. This was effective for years on the gridiron and also during the crime, considering the fact that while he was brutally attacking one person, he had to manage to elude another at the same time. Simpson had a long stride and excellent vision, enabling him to find openings in the defense and exploit them effectively. This was also apparent during and after killing people. Not only did he need to envision how he would escape the crime scene while committing the murder of two people, he had to execute that escape quickly. He possessed exceptional footwork, enabling him to make sharp cuts and dodge defenders with subtle shifts in direction. This is largely why he broke the single-season rushing record in 1973, and why he was able to get back to his mansion in just a few minutes.

Overall, Simpson's running style was characterized by its elegance, power, and effectiveness, making him one of the most dominant running backs in the history of American football... it also made him one of the most effective double murderers we've ever witnessed.

There's just no other criminal athlete that could match what Simpson did.

Aaron Hernandez's stats are close to Simpson's, but he was never the athlete Simpson was, and wasn't a killer nearly as crafty as Simpson. It's not even close. Some may disagree. Hernandez killed at least one, likely two people, and there is very strong evidence he killed more. The problem with this is that unconfirmed killings are still unconfirmed. On top of that, Hernandez didn't even come close to a "not guilty" verdict. He was done the minute he was arrested. "Not guilty" was never even an option. If we look at this with zero bias, we also could argue that O.J. killed other people we don't know about, and the ones we do know about for sure are still more than Hernandez. Couple that with the fact that Simpson somehow snowed twelve people into believing he didn't do it, and it's no longer even debatable. Hernandez isn't even in the conversation.

Ray Lewis was involved in the death of two people stabbed outside of an Atlanta club in 2000, but it's unclear if he did it or not. Initial reports from witnesses suggested that Lewis was involved, but later those accounts changed. By most accounts, Lewis didn't stab anyone. The charges filed against him were obstruction of justice. Did he actually stab people to death? Well, that's complicated, but not likely, and even if he did, it would have been just one guy at best. On top of this, his own handling of his charges wasn't nearly as clean. Take a look at the tape. There was less evidence that Lewis actually stabbed two people versus Simpson, yet he was willing to plea bargain if the deal had no jail time and was reduced to a misdemeanor or changed to some kind of self-defense plea. Simpson, on the other hand, clearly was guilty with a ton of evidence pointing right at him, but never even flinched with a plea bargain. He said, "I didn't do it," with balls of steel and, somehow, just like he avoided so many defenders on the field, juked the fuck out of a "guilty" verdict.

The jaws that dropped to the floor during his playing days were only matched on the day the verdict was read. Doesn't matter if it was the 1970s or 1995, no one could touch him and no one could bring him down.

Lawrence Phillips, Sergio Brown, Darren Sharper, Kellen Winslow Jr., Rae Carruth… it doesn't matter who it is. All of them are scrubs compared to Simpson. Not only did they fail to even come close to the greatness Simpson displayed on the field, they also never could match the effectiveness and ruthlessness Simpson displayed off the field.

If there was a Hall of Fame for Criminal Athletes, O.J. Simpson would be a first-ballot hall of famer and the all-time GOAT. Well, actually… that may not be the case. If there was a place to put the greatest athlete criminals the world has ever seen, we all know O.J. would somehow get out of it.

# The Weird Things You'll Find While Apartment Hunting

Finding an apartment is hard work, not like I imagined it would be when I first got my own place at 19 years old back in the mid-1990s. Over the years, I rented a lot of places, so I have become an expert in how to find a nice place to live with minimal headache.

This is important now, more than ever, with rent costs going through the roof and good spots getting harder to find. Yes… you can still find a great place that is affordable and in a desirable area if you know what you're doing. I'm here to offer you some advice on how to do just that.

Most folks striking out on their own for the first time often make the mistake of assuming that finding an apartment is easy, especially since most people who move say things like, "I just got a new place," with an easiness in their voice. It sounds simple enough. They almost never complain about the experience or simply choose not to talk about it… I really don't know. I never listen to what people say. Most of the time my brain is consumed with random pointless thoughts, old songs, or I'm thinking about sex.

Let's not get distracted here.

The point is this: It's not as easy as people say it is, nor as easy as I assume because I never listen. Either way, most folks will discover the hard way that finding an apartment is about as enjoyable as getting punched in the face by Mike Tyson for 60 minutes. But then again, that would only last 60 minutes.

Here are some pointers to help you find your perfect place and to minimize the headache.

The first thing you will learn about your search for an apartment is that there is so much more to it than just finding the right place for the right price. There are steps to follow, guidelines, and rules.

First and foremost, you'll need to pick up all the clothes and classic albums your girlfriend threw out into the street. Also, get your smartphone. She will keep it because it's linked to the bank accounts she will attempt to drain, and it also has the phone number of the woman who is partly responsible for you trying to find that limited-edition Flock of Seagulls album underneath your neighbor's Honda Civic.

Let's face it: this is really about location at the top of the priority list. Most people will compromise on price if the location is nice. Rule number one: If you can hear rap music blaring from the parking lot of the apartment complex while you're still three blocks away, skip to the next complex. Also, never move into a place where your neighbor's name contains words like "Dawg," "Loc," "Shorty," or "Dre," unless you know they are an established rap star and not just the "cousin" of one, or a guy that claims to be "huge on the Internet."

This also goes for any place near an area with a high concentration of buffets. If you see a lot of restaurants that offer all-you-can-eat, then it's likely that most folks who live in that area have toilet paper with headlines and weather reports printed on them. The key is to look for places where the house can move, but the ten cars on the property don't. Keep a keen eye open for the folks that return from the dump with more junk than they took, and look out for any middle schools with daycare centers.

These are places you want to avoid. So, how do we find a great location?

Ads on any college campus are a good place to start. College students can provide hookups for new friends. It also offers the chance to meet drunken coeds and convince them that you're a 25-year-old grad student and not some 35-year-old guy that works at NAPA Auto Parts part time.

Also, the Internet has become a great place for people looking to find a place. Many websites and social media apps are dedicated to helping those wanting to connect with others, including those looking for a place to live. Not only can you easily find plenty of places and rooms that are available for rent, these websites and apps also connect us with people looking to be defecated on, to join an orgy, those interested in being involved in gang bangs, and other limitless opportunities to be humiliated in a sexual encounter.

Maybe you decide to get your own place and skip the roommate thing.

If you decide that you want your own place, always meet with the landlord before signing the lease. This is important not just because you need to meet the guy who will be taking your rent, but also to get a sense of whether or not he's the kind of guy who will put hidden cameras everywhere or sneak into your apartment while you're at work to sniff your underwear.

If you go this route, be prepared financially because landlords often request unexpected things, such as a deposit equal to the first month's rent. This is known as "prick money." Also, be prepared to spend some money cleaning because the "prick money" he took from the previous tenants was mostly used to buy booze, ended up in the G-strings of strippers, or was spent at Posh Sensations Massage Parlor, which is definitely not a front for prostitutes.

One other thing to keep in mind about landlords is their tendency to try and play you like you're some kind of chump. Let them know up front that you're not some kind of chump.

Also, you need to be aware of places that sound like they're really cool, because they may not be what you expect. Here's what I mean. For a short time I lived above "The Owl's Nest," a bar in Oakland. Living above a bar might seem cool, but there were a few things I wasn't expecting to deal with.

First, just because I don't go out to the bars every night until 2 a.m. doesn't mean others don't. I felt like I was the Siamese twin of an alcoholic that thought "Freebird" was the only song ever recorded. Just a quick note: check out the jukebox before signing the lease. You will be hearing those songs over and over again.

Second, just because a bar closes at 2 a.m. doesn't mean everyone goes home. The owner of the bar may regularly hold small intimate get-togethers with a few friends after hours, which is usually no big deal… or they may have a cocaine-fueled after-hours party where it sounds like the Super Bowl Halftime Show under your bed.

Hint: It's usually the latter.

Even before you go out to look at a place, learn what certain terms actually mean. If the ad reads that it's "close to public transportation," this means that it's "close to people who use public transportation." If it says it's "close to the freeway," that means it's close to those who "live under the freeway."

See where I'm going with this?

Terms like "charming" and "historic neighborhood" can mean a number of things. "Charming" can mean you'll rent a walk-in closet, or it can mean you're going to be living with an 80-year-old woman who wears see-through nightgowns and quotes *Matlock*… or both. "Historic neighborhood" means that the crackheads, heroin addicts, and homeless alcoholics have been there for years, possibly decades, while the drug dealers and gangs have likely been there for multiple generations.

Let's not even get into "up-and-coming" neighborhoods.

Lastly, let's talk about home ownership. Many folks want to buy a house and not rent, even if they are fairly new to the world of finding their own place. While not the most common route for folks first leaving the nest, buying a home immediately after moving out of your parents' place, or after renting for only a short time, does happen.

However, Generation Z and Gen Alpha say this option is off the table, claiming they face an expensive housing market that has outpaced pay for most jobs. This isn't really 100 percent accurate. Many cities in America have always been too expensive for most jobs, especially big cities and areas with nice weather.

The question really is this: Is it generally more expensive now, and is housing simply out of reach for younger folks? I would say yes and no. It is out of reach in more places than ever before, but that doesn't mean you can't grind harder and smarter to obtain a home or widen your net to find towns and cities that are still very affordable. We did it, our parents did it, and their parents did it. It was never easy, even if it was easier back then.

Point is this: I'm getting sick of Generation Z and Millennials with their "know-it-all," entitled attitudes. They keep bitching about a system they claim is rigged against them. You want to see serious real estate inflation? Go rent a bounce house. Kids today… they're always walking around acting like they rent the place.

Good luck in your search.

# The Six Habits of the Highly Average, and How You Can Be Highly Average Too

For many adults, their life could be described as less than average. In many cases, it could be a downright failure. Folks typically point to things like one's childhood, other similar circumstances or experiences throughout their life, luck of the draw, lack of opportunity, drug or alcohol use, or simply laziness as reasons why someone ends up at the bottom of the professional and social ladders.

However, that can change… and I know for a fact it can change for everyone. No matter who you are or your circumstances, it can get better, and I'm here with some suggestions that can help you excel in life. Now, can you be highly successful? Sure… but you also could win the lottery on the same day NASA recruits you for the first mission to Mars. What I'm saying is let's stay focused on reality.

At best, I think you could be highly average.

Unlike Tony Robbins, Tai Lopez, Grant Cardone, or any other questionable guru that keeps repeating the same motivational clichés, peddling suspect courses, and selling you the dream that you can be highly successful, I'm not here to bullshit you.

I see who you are. I know you… and let me say this: I'm not impressed.

So, let's get real… but also, let's get real motivated too; just do it within reason. Don't ever settle for anything less than what 100 percent of your mental drive and dedication can bring to you. I have seen your 100 percent, and it's about 25 percent of those who are actually successful. Bottom line: Never settle for anything less than being highly average, which is about as much as we can hope for in your case.

Now, what if you achieve mediocrity and master that? Then can you work toward being highly successful? Whoa… slow your roll. Even the average version of you at your peak is still quite unlikable and lacks any real intellectual capacity, charm, wit, or charisma.

Let's not get carried away.

The first thing we need to do is discuss the six habits of the highly average and visualize how you can get there.

1.) The highly average exhibit just a slight lack of personal responsibility.

People with a highly average drive, mentality, and behavior sometimes point a finger at others, but not always. They sometimes come up with excuses for what happens and why it happens to them. Some say it's a desire to avoid facing any real pressure and to skate by, doing just enough to not get fired. However, despite this, average people pick and choose these spots carefully. You, on the other hand, don't do any of this. Your entire life is one big excuse. You never skate by, but rather are dragged across the road of life facedown, while even the most basic responsibilities treat you like a heavy bag at the gym.

It's time to man up and grab that average life by the horns. For example, wake up before 10 a.m., and instead of masturbating all morning, try taking a shower and getting outside to find something productive to do… no, I don't mean go to GameStop or to the park to meet up with that Russian model you've wired airfare to, claiming she'll come see you.

2.) Highly average folks only procrastinate.

Highly average folks delay their work, and when they're even slightly successful, they take that win and rest on their laurels for as long as they can. However, the takeaway is they *still get it done*. You, on the other hand, do not procrastinate. You simply don't do shit. Deadlines are either an enigma to you, or it's a word that might as well be sesquipedalian: you don't know what it means, nor do you care.

If you want to be highly average, you have to break that habit. You need to develop the skill of blowing off shit *only until the last minute*, versus never doing it at all. Start small. Like doing your laundry this week instead of… well… never, like your usual routine of doing nothing. Build from there. Look around your house. Consider all the shit you've never done, which is just about everything… because you never do shit.

What I'm saying is this: Try anything at all, and try it before the end of the week.

3.) Highly average folks have a touch of the "why me" mentality.

People who are highly average sometimes have a "why me" mentality. Sometimes this can be minor, or it could be a big meltdown. Regardless, they have it sometimes. Generally speaking, however, this is in passing and often nothing more than an eruption in the moment. They'll get over it and move on. It's temporary.

You, however, live the "why me" 24/7, and the only trigger you need is to be breathing and the day on the calendar to change. This is all it takes for you to start bitching... well, to *continue* bitching. To actually start bitching, you'd have to stop at some point.

4.) Highly average people are sometimes defensive.

The highly average are sometimes defensive, but this is usually only when they honestly believe they are being treated or blamed unfairly. They also may act this way if someone is laying blame on them while not taking any of the blame themselves. They wouldn't see this as being defensive, but rather others blaming them to escape their own failures.

You, on the other hand, get defensive at nearly anything said to you. It could be something relevant, like a person asking you, "Is this your fault?" or a comment that wasn't something to be defensive about in the first place, such as, "Do you happen to know what time it is?" Either way, you lash out defensively at just about everything. You're so deeply insecure that even someone asking you for the time of day feels like an insult. It reminds you of what you're doing at that time of day… which is nothing… and since you don't do shit all day, every day, no matter what time of the day it is when someone asks you, it comes across as insulting.

The best way to avoid being defensive is to actually follow through, which will steer you clear of any accusations. This means relevant work, *not* completing levels on *Call of Duty* or arguing successfully online that a tomato would win in a fight against an onion if both vegetables were sentient. You see where I'm going with this?

5.) They set mid-level expectations.

Highly average folks set the bar somewhere in the middle. They're not the best, but never the worst. You, on the other hand, set the bar low on your best days. Most of the time you don't even set a bar. In fact, I would argue that no matter how low it is set, you would still find some way to avoid crossing it. What I'm saying is this: You're so lazy you would suffocate if breathing wasn't a natural bodily function. If you were required to act on breathing, that would be too much effort for you.

I'm actually surprised you don't starve to death. Food, even at its minimum, requires you to open a refrigerator or cabinet door and then open a package. That's two whole steps requiring you to do something, and it's clear you do at least that. You're still alive. Maybe there is hope for you after all.

6.) Highly average folks hang out with people like them.

The highly average hang with the highly average, which is why they are highly average. You will likely be at the same professional and social level as the folks you hang out with. This is probably the most important move you can make to be more than you are… and since you are an indifferent and lackadaisical washout who is bordering on comatose, we have nowhere to go but up.

Your first problem is the people you hang out with are all online, and there is no lower form of friends than that. The good news is friends online don't really impact your ability to rise up, at least not like your friends in real life do. The problem is that you have no friends in real life. This is both good and bad news. First, the good news: If you have no friends, you don't have losers dragging you down. The bad news: The only real person that hangs out with you is you… and you're useless, so you're starting in a negative position. Now, what are the odds of you meeting folks in higher social and professional positions? That's 100 percent guaranteed. Everyone is doing better than you, so they're easy to find. However, what are the odds they'll want to be around you? It's zero.

Look at this whole situation as the glass is half full… but in your case, it isn't getting any fuller. Always understand that being highly average is a choice, and you have a choice to advance to that level… well, maybe in your case you really don't have a choice, but in theory you do. Again, that's in theory, which is at least something.

# Famous Movie Quotes for Awkward Social Situations

Over the past 10 years, I have found myself climbing the social ladder to heights I never would have thought possible. What started as a venture into investing and real estate has led me to social circles I would never have imagined being involved in. I've learned a lot… but the most shocking thing I learned was something I wasn't expecting.

Rich folks are really fucking weird.

I'm talking about folks who either were born rich or have been rich for so long they have totally forgotten what normal people are like. Now, for me, I've been on every rung of the socioeconomic ladder. I lived in trailer parks as a kid, moved into middle class, then into upper-middle class, and ended up quite wealthy by my mid-30s. Now, in my mid-40s, I have been entrenched in elite circles for a decade. I've lived all these lives at one time or another, so I have a firm grasp on the concepts of social construction, norms, and expectations in every socioeconomic circle.

However, sometimes I'm still put in awkward social situations where I'm left speechless. This could happen in any social situation, but it seems to happen more often in elite circles. To deal with awkward situations, I have adopted the practice of using movie quotes when people say odd or strange things that either make me very uncomfortable or put me in a place where I have no idea how to respond. It has paid dividends.

Here are a few examples.

One night at a party, a man who I had just met ten minutes prior dumped some heavy personal news on me. I don't even know this dude. Why is he telling me this? The only response that came to mind was a famous quote from the movie *Forrest Gump*.

"Sean, I just got some test results back from my doctor, and I have cancer."

"Mama always said life was like a box of chocolates. You never know what you're gonna get."

He hugged me. Either he found my response profound or he really loves that film. Regardless, the hug just made things weirder.

My neighbor is a very successful doctor, but he also is a bit of a blockhead in many ways. When presented with an obvious scam perpetrated by a social-proofing fraudster, everyone around him knew it, but he was convinced otherwise, despite what everyone was telling him. He lost a lot of money and was kicking himself because he didn't listen to anyone when they warned him.

What was I going to say? He was the only person in our social circle who fell for this, so the "it could happen to anyone" line wasn't going to work, because it didn't happen to anyone else. He couldn't believe he was that stupid, but we all did.

"I still can't understand why I did such an idiotic thing by investing with that guy. Y'all told me he was a charlatan, and part of me had suspicions, but the proof was there. He had the cars, the mansion, the plane, the documentation… everything. You all tried to warn me that it was rented and faked, and couldn't believe I was this stupid. What can I say? I now have to agree with you guys. I can't believe I was that stupid."

I just thought of Sean Maguire from the movie *Good Will Hunting*.

"Some people can't believe in themselves until someone else believes in them first."

Then there are the folks deep into cryptocurrency. It's the wild west out there, and most projects are scams. I've been warning folks for years, but many just don't seem to listen. Because they have a ton of money, they believe they know how to make a ton of money.

Newsflash: Just because you're on third base doesn't mean you hit a triple. Get it?

I had to deal with my friend Elliot who put his entire savings into FTX, something I highly advised against.

"You were right about crypto investing, Sean. I can't believe I invested everything into FTX."

After warning him and criticizing him, what the hell was I going to say? Tyler Durden from *Fight Club* instantly popped into my head.

"It's only after we've lost everything that we're free to do anything."

One of my fellow members at the local country club got popped for some insider trading and suddenly was in a world he didn't know: jail. As the law closed in, they dropped several felony charges on him, and he was looking at a quarter century. He took a deal quick, but the deal itself wasn't that great either. This dude was going to prison for a long time, regardless.

"So, I took a ten-year prison sentence deal. Better than facing 25 years if I went to trial, right?"

Nah, bruh. I would have tried another route, another lawyer, or even taken my chances at trial. A decade in prison? What the fuck was I going to say to this? *The Lion King* quickly popped into my head.

"It's important to always look where you're headed rather than where you were."

Now, I know what you're thinking. This isn't so awkward... and I actually agree with you. This is tame compared to other situations. These are the easy conversations. Shit gets way more uncomfortable than this.

My neighbor's daughter was discussing with me how her dad was pushing her to go to college, something she really didn't want to do. His response to her was to either go to school or go to work. However, she didn't want to work if it wasn't going to pay well, so she started bouncing ideas off me about career paths that pay highly but require little skill.

"I'm thinking about either trying an OnlyFans account or even possibly trying to get into the porn industry. What do you think?"

Holy shit. What the fuck was I going to say to her? Blowjobs are a great career move? I was shocked, and the only thing that came out of my mouth was a quote from Yoda.

"Do, or do not. There is no 'try.'"

It only gets more personal when another friend got burned by his own brother, financially and emotionally, and I told him to cut the guy out completely, which he didn't like me suggesting.

"Fire him? That's my brother. I don't care that he embezzled millions from me and stole my wife. I just can't throw family out of my life. What kind of advice is that?"

He seemed upset at what I said, and Jules Winnfield from *Pulp Fiction* was the only thing I had to offer.

"If my answers frighten you, then you should cease asking scary questions."

However, sometimes shit got so fucking strange and twisted that even Hollywood couldn't really save me. The quotes just became a knee-jerk response to shit so fucking far out there that a legitimate response didn't exist, even if I wanted to give one. Again, I can't stress this enough: Rich people are wrapped up in seriously weird and warped shit all the time.

"Look, I really need your help on this, Sean. My wife and I are basically done, but I can't afford the divorce because she'll wipe me out. Frankly, I don't want a divorce. I love my wife... well, I love things about her, I should say. I mean, I am seeing another woman too, who I also don't want to leave. The problem there is that I'm also having an affair with my mistress's sister. I'm done with the sister, but I'm trying to keep her from talking and ruining things with my mistress, who then might rat me out to my wife. I'm trying to figure out what to do with all of this, and I'm just looking for some advice. You're one of the smartest men I know."

What the fuck are you asking of me? Is there a human on this planet who could offer you any sound advice in this situation? Out of nowhere, my brain went straight to Mary Crawford from *Mansfield Park*.

"You think if you shake me hard enough something profound will come out, but I assure you, I am profoundly shallow."

Same shit happened just a few days later with another acquaintance from work. I barely know this dude, but he dumped all of his emotional shit on me.

"I know we fight all the time, but I love her. I guess it doesn't seem that way, since we're always bickering. I don't like the fact that she doesn't work, but I'm making enough money to support us, as long as she keeps her cocaine use to a minimum. But then when she cuts back on coke, she hits the bottle pretty hard. These are really the main problems. I don't care about the cheating.

I cheated too. Granted, she had sex with my son, and I only did her best friend. Not even blood-related. Let's get real. That's not even as bad as your son. No one is going to argue that."

What? I don't even know where to start with this. I'm not sure I even understand it. All that popped in my head was the famous quote from the film *Airplane*.

"Looks like I picked the wrong week to quit sniffing glue."

Normally, I wouldn't lean on Hollywood for anything. However, I realized this works because Hollywood is fiction… and if any group of people on this planet lives in a fabricated and unreal world, it's rich people. Remember, they don't do what they do for the money… they do it for a shitload of money.

What? You didn't think I could find a spot for a *Spaceballs* quote?

# I Can Tell What Kind of White Trash You Are By Your Choice in Buffets

Growing up in a trailer park, I lived the life of my poor white brethren, which encompassed a lot of the stereotypes many folks hear about rednecks. At the time, it only seemed a bit odd to me. My mother and father, both attending college at the time, were living in this place because of financial struggles, not because they were actually rednecks themselves. However, living in a trailer park, barely getting by, led my family to practice much of the same rituals of the white trash world.

This included the weekly night out to dinner at the buffet.

Put on your nicest shirt, which basically meant to find one with sleeves, then head out with the family for some one-star dining. Some of my earliest memories were of these magical restaurants that allow you to eat all you can. To add to the magic, these places often had every type of food under the sun.

You want pizza? We got that... like 25 kinds of pizza. It sits right next to the Mexican food section, just behind the omelet station. Yeah, that's right, we serve breakfast all fuckin' day and night too. You like Chinese? It's all you can eat and dim sum.

By the time I was ten, I was fully bought into the enchantment of filling up a full plate with broccoli beef... nothing but broccoli beef... then more broccoli beef. If I was still hungry, I would just get more broccoli beef… and no motherfucker could stop me.

I will break your fucking wok before I leave this place.

My brother saw this whole journey as a competition. A way to rip off the restaurant. He always had this attitude like, "These bitches are going to regret ever letting me step foot into this place." We were kids… what the fuck did we know? We got excited over our school cafeteria's square-cut pizza, so these buffets seemed gourmet to us.

As I got older and our family moved out of the trailer park into a more affluent existence, I noticed something: The food at buffets wasn't really all that good, and most of the people in the restaurant seemed familiar, but somehow different. I kept thinking that most of these folks probably have been assaulted with a toilet seat at least once in their life.

The first time this all dawned on me was Christmas break of my eighth-grade year. It was the day I realized I was white trash… and also the day I realized I was no longer white trash. By the time I was 18, I had fully grown out of these shit-bag establishments, but my brother was still into buffets. By this point, our old mutual childhood love for these places turned into a regular argument. He defended these joints, while I argued that the ability to swap out the buns of a hamburger for two chicken fried steaks doesn't make you Gordon Ramsay, nor does it make the sandwich you just created a five-star Michelin dish.

Look, just because a buffet allows you to turn your dinner into an arts-and-crafts project doesn't make the food any better.

My brother, however, found a new place that had just opened in our hometown: Golden Corral. He swore to me that this place was different. For the first time, he had found a buffet restaurant that was head and shoulders above all others. Call it nostalgia for a simpler time, or his obnoxious ranting that made me give in just to shut him up, or the five beers I slammed that afternoon, but I was in.

I learned a few things on this inaugural trip to Golden Corral: One, the food was better than every other buffet restaurant I ever frequented. Two, the food was still shit. Three, the people there were just a slightly higher-class version of the same hayseed yokels me and my brother grew up around.

I also learned that I could now tell what kind of white trash someone is by the buffet restaurants they patronized.

The worst buffet I ever went to was CiCi's. It's a national buffet pizza chain that somehow managed to make pizza nearly inedible. How is this even possible? Pizza is like sex: Even when it's bad, it's still pretty good. CiCi's should be commended for this achievement. The ability to completely fuck up pizza to this degree is really an accomplishment. At the end of the day, you've done something that very few, if any, have ever done. It's not something to be proud of, but you are the best at it.

If CiCi's is your spot of choice, you probably missed your eighth-grade graduation because you had jury duty, and you keep a can of Raid on your kitchen table next to the salt and pepper shakers. I can't wrap my head around why anyone would frequent this place regularly, but a lot of people must, because they are still open. I assume it's the type of person that believes they have a personalized license plate because a relative actually made the plate.

Shoney's is another place that I went to often, and even as a kid, thought there was a problem. It's a national chain, mostly in the South, and the food has a unique quality that I have never seen before. The food looks like it's been sitting out for days, even if it was just brought out. Seriously… they could physically walk out of the kitchen, set it up for the buffet, and it already looks like it's been sitting out since last Tuesday. Much like CiCi's, to pull something off this monumentally bad is both disturbing and impressive at the same time. How is it possible for you to bring out four freshly cooked batches of food and it immediately looks like the cast of *The Golden Girls*?

However, this place would be packed, mostly by folks whose dinnerware probably has names like Cool Whip and Daisy Sour Cream written on the side, and those who use the broken television as a stand for the TV that works. In Shoney's defense, I think they also have a regular menu, functioning like a traditional restaurant, which may be better food… but in the 1980s, when I was a kid, I don't recall that. It was just a buffet, and a bad one at that.

Hometown Buffet, another national chain that also goes by several other names, is terrible, but not as bad as CiCi's or Shoney's. However, that isn't saying much. The food tastes like the failed sibling of a successful person. What does that mean? Imagine having a great piece of chicken at some restaurant. Hometown Buffet would have that chicken's unfortunate sibling that, in some ways, exhibited a lot of potential in the beginning, but ultimately became a paste eater that couldn't color within the lines, spending the bulk of their adult years telling everyone they were aggressively applying for jobs online when they were really just jerking off to porn most of the day.

You see where I'm going with this?

The food seems to have potential, but then it ultimately disappoints you. It's garbage, but it seemed like it could have been a contender… and much like the failed sibling of someone successful, you cannot quite figure out how it ended up this way. People that eat at Hometown Buffet care about their food choices, care about quality, and aren't afraid to go the extra mile for something a little nicer. Problem is, they're too stupid to know what that exactly means, and that's why they end up at Hometown Buffet. You see, the failed brother of the family still looks a lot like success to those that think a Magic 8 Ball's response to money management is a great way to invest a stimulus check.

Now, if you're high class, you hit Sizzler and Golden Corral. However, those that go to these places are the worst of the bunch. It's like they're smart enough to know these are the best buffet spots, but still dumb enough to think that a buffet spot could actually be any good.

This is very frustrating.

How about going to a real restaurant, for God's sake? Go to a place where people actually serve you. Where you have to order and specify how you want your food cooked. A place that has menus and a bar with glasses instead of plastic cups. Look, I'm not making fun of these folks at all, because I lived this exact life too. I was raised in a trailer park. A place so run down that a tornado would cause $50,000 in improvements to our home. My first dream job was owning a fireworks stand, and my dad used a rag as a gas cap. Why do you think we went to these buffets so much as kids?

The fact is these restaurants will always have a strong clientele, and that's great, for both the businesses and the customers that enjoy these dining experiences. I'm happy for both. Despite my own commentary, I think these restaurants are really great family destinations. No, I'm not suddenly changing my mind about these places. However, no one takes their family to buffets for the food; they take their family there to have an evening out with their family. The food sucks, but those times as a child with the ones you love are amazing and can magically make any food taste better... even CiCi's pizza.

# No One Cares About Your Social Media Politics… We Just Want Cats or Titties

Social media had a basic design when it first emerged in the early 2000s: connect people and share their lives while, at the same time, giving these folks the power to interact with each other through this virtual gathering of friends and relatives.

It was all supposed to be simple, lighthearted, and positive… until it wasn't.

It's hard to deny that social media is no longer this unadulterated playground. It's now the hub for drama, mostly sparked by cursory political rhetoric and angry ideological twits who come off as pompous jerks. Let's face it… social media is now the home of the most superficial, self-righteous, and condescending political commentary you will ever find, with the added hand claps between words to make it even more insufferable.

"Okay, it's really this simple. Stop talking and pay attention: In the 1990s, Homer Simpson supported his family on a single-income union job and owned a home, all with just a high school education. That isn't possible today. DO YOU GET IT YET!!??"

Seriously? *The Simpsons* as evidence to support an argument about the current wealth gap in America? My God… it's a fucking cartoon, you arrogant imbecile. They're not real. Before you launch your verbal attack on me, stop for a moment and let me clue you in on something you need to know.

No one on social media cares about your politics; they just want to see cats or titties.

Really, that's it.

No one on social media gives a fuck if you're a Democrat, Republican, some third-party supporter, or an independent. Stop spamming your social media feeds with flimsy and biased memes that absolutely no one on this planet cares about.

Folks want to see funny cats doing hilarious shit... or some titties. This is what social media is best suited to offer us and what most of us want to see.

Look, don't get me wrong, talking about politics is extremely important. However, this must be done in a different environment, like in person, sitting together and discussing facts, ideas, constructs, situations, nuances, and history. That's where it belongs, not in the current social media environment.

Seriously, ask yourself when you see these posts on your feed: Who are these people posting this garbage for? Are they seriously thinking they're going to change anyone's mind? Or that someone out there is on the fence about an issue and their intellectually hollow meme is going to tip the scale? You're a 20-year-old student at the local community college taking *Philosophy of Reality Television* and *Art Appreciation*. You're still enraged about that episode where Homer Simpson's white privilege landed him on a space shuttle mission, despite being horribly unqualified.

Stay in your lane, Scooter.

Fact is, even if someone agrees with whatever you posted, they're not going to agree with the way you present it or the way you present yourself. The pretension is just the first nauseating part of your personality. Top that off with your depthless and empty intellect, which is more concerned with feuding online, and your whole persona becomes that of a childish, ignorant malcontent whose only skill is to draw other lightweights into a downward spiral of disagreement.

All of these platforms are just littered with a bunch of one-dimensional rabid dogs barking at each other to see who can be the loudest simpleton in the room. No one is actually trying to have a discussion; it's just trendy to post some desultory meme you think is intellectually deep simply to upset some other halfwit who will respond with his gibberish. It's why social media is such a God-damn cancer. We need to hit the reset button and go back to what these platforms do best: hilarious cats… and titties.

I know that regardless of what I say, folks will argue that social media politics, even if it's superficial and shallow, is still more important and relevant than cats or titties, but they're horribly misguided, and I disagree wholeheartedly. You see, those cats and titties are real… Homer Simpson isn't.

# I Invited Two Jehovah's Witnesses Into My House

I think every American, regardless of their background, has universal experiences. Things like falling in love, joy, disappointment, dreams, fears, and, of course, Jehovah's Witnesses coming to your home.

It's a rite of passage for every American to hear that knock at the door, deal with these folks who are delivering the good news, and choose your preferred response of rejection. This is everything from a soft "No thanks," to the avoidance response of "I'm sorry, but I'm another religion," to the hardcore "Fuck off." That's just the start. There are a million creative ways of telling them you're about as interested in their religion as you are in getting a terminal illness.

Whatever you wish to say, it's open game. It's like a real-life version of the joke "The Aristocrats." Seriously, go as hard as you want. For me, I've done them all. It got to the point where I was constantly trying to come up with new ways to tell them I wasn't interested.

"Hey, have you guys thought of opening a religious-based gym? You would have a captive audience. Call it Jehovah's Fitness."

I know… it's really gotten out of hand.

So, earlier this month, I was eating my Corn Flakes and watching YouTube videos of people getting bit by snakes. You know, typical morning. Suddenly, there was a knock at the door. I'll admit, I wasn't ready for this. I didn't order DoorDash, escort services don't open this early, and I have no family or friends that ever visit unless I owe them money. Then it clicked. I knew what I was dealing with.

Fucking Jehovah's Witnesses. I answered the door, and right away they started in with their spiel.

"Excuse me, sir. Do you have a moment to talk about the Lord and Savior?"

Instantly, dozens of responses came to mind. However, I've used most of these responses before, and the new material racing through my head in that moment seemed stale. It was still just the same kind of shit. I had been there, done that. I could drop a million different responses, but I had played that game at the highest level. By this point in my life, I'm the Michael Jordan/LeBron James hybrid of telling these folks to go fuck themselves. I had to take the game to the next level. I said something no one else would ever think to say:

"Sure, come in… let's talk about the Lord and Savior."

These two guys didn't say a word as they walked into my house, and that was awkward, so I tried to break the ice a bit with a joke. This was tricky, admittedly, because I do not know that much about their specific brand of Christianity, so jokes weren't poppin' off in my head. In fact, the only thing I understand is that many

Christians don't think Jehovah's Witnesses are Christians at all, despite their claims that they are Christians.

Whatever, I had to say something to ease the tension.

"I'm not sure I can be a Jehovah's Witness. I didn't see the accident."

That joke was met with crickets as both young men looked at me, confused. They didn't get it at all. That's fine. They're in good company. I don't know shit about their religion. They're confused. I'm confused. It's all good. It's organized religion, after all, which is mostly unorganized.

Both were carrying folders, but it was unclear what was in them. I assumed it was some literature that advertised whatever it is they're preaching, but these two guys still hadn't said one word, so here I was staring at their materials like some asshole.

"What is it you've got there? Are those free Jehovah's Witness calendars?"

The two guys were perplexed.

"What do you mean by calendars?"

"You know, like they hand out at the bank. Each month has some kind of theme to it. At my bank, it's usually a different cat each month… or something like that."

I looked at them for confirmation, but I'm not sure they understood why I was asking such a stupid and random question. Fair enough. I wasn't sure why I was asking such a stupid and random question either.

"What pictures would be in those calendars? Is it a different color door being slammed in your face each month?"

That joke landed like the Hindenburg.

I poured three cups of coffee and offered some to my guests. I then asked them to have a seat on the sofa. Before I allowed these guys to start with their spiel, I wanted to lay some foundation out for them. I needed them to know where I was coming from. I had to be real with myself and face the fact that no matter what these dudes said, there was virtually no way I was ever going to join up with this religion.

"So, in full disclosure, I'm not sure I can be a true Jehovah's Witness… maybe a Jehovah's Observer."

"I'm sorry. What is that exactly?" one guy asked.

"It's like a Jehovah's Witness, but we don't get involved."

"I'm sorry, sir, but that isn't a real thing."

They seemed a bit annoyed at my ignorance. At this point, I had little choice left but to simply get on with this presentation. The two young men settled in and I attempted to be as serious as possible, giving them my full attention and open-mindedness. This was no longer a joke. I wanted to hear what they had to say and if they could convince me to consider the path of becoming a Jehovah's Witness.

The ball is in your court, boys. Convert me.

There was a moment of silence. The two young men nervously thumbed through their folders and looked at each other, seemingly confused, as if each expected the other to start the dialogue.

"Well, guys… what is it that you want to share with me? I'm all ears."

"We don't know what to tell you," one of the men said sheepishly.

"What do you mean you don't know what to tell me?"

"I mean we don't know what to say at this point. We've never made it this far."

That was that… they left. What a waste of time, and I didn't even get a calendar.

So what did I learn from this? I learned that if a Jehovah's Witness starts a knock-knock joke, they'll likely never get an answer, and you shouldn't volunteer to give them one. I also learned we're not all that much different at the end of the day. Sure, I have no religious background and spent my life attending the school of hard knocks, not church. However, I realized that these dudes also went to the school of hard knocks as well. Don't believe me? Just ask every neighbor on my block. They'll tell you all about it.

# I Love You DoorDash, but We Need to Take Step Back On Our Relationship

I still love everything about us, and I will always cherish our time together, but I think it's time to move on, DoorDash. You know it too… I guess I'm just the one to say it first.

The convenience, the cuisine, the quick delivery time, and that smile I know you flashed under that mask every time you handed me my food… I'll never forget any of it. Italy, China, Mexico, Japan, and many others. We've traveled the world together… in terms of the type of food you delivered to me. All of them memorable. I'll never forget that Peking duck from China's Great Wall Cafe or the Banderias Pilche from Cantina De Zacatecas. Even the time I ordered a pizza from Richie's New York Slices and the toppings were wrong, but I ended up liking it more than the one I ordered.

It was always like that with you. Even the wrong orders were glorious journeys, more so because they were unexpected.

Truly fantastic.

However, all of this has changed. I first got the feeling something was wrong when I stopped seeing you as often. You started to drift away. We used to see each other all the time, then only every few orders or so… but now I don't see you at all. You just leave my food at the door and don't even knock.

Also, I noticed on my app that you go to so many other houses before you come over. I understand… you have other orders, but now you go to those places before me. I used to always be first, or at least second. Now? I'm at the bottom of the list. You know how unimportant that makes me feel?

But it's when you started denying my orders that I knew this relationship was coming to an end. Was it the changes in me over the last few months? I know I used to just order from a few places on this side of town, but I have grown, and my tastes have matured, like getting the Empadão with a side of Brigadeiro from the Cantinho Moqueca Brazilian Grill. I get it… they are all the way on the other side of the city, but they are the only ones that serve Brazilian cuisine. I thought you would always be by my side, growing together. I guess we just want different things out of life.

In the end, it's clear our relationship comes down to the fact that financially it's just not working anymore. Not just for you, but for me too. That's why I think things have been the way they've been lately. You're awesome, and you're worth being showered with everything you deserve and want, but I just don't make the kind of money to keep this relationship going with all the increases in gas, added app fees, and expected raises in tips. I can only give you what I can, and it's not enough to make you happy.

I have been holding on for too long and lying to myself that it wasn't over, but I needed to finally make a clean break. Deleting my DoorDash app was necessary for me to finally let go of the delusion that things would change.

I thought about signing up with Uber Eats, but I'm not sure I'm ready to jump back into something like this right away. I need time to myself. To work on myself. I don't want to be hurt again.

# My Rejection Letter from a Very Big Online Satire Publication

Thank you for your interest in our publication, but unfortunately, we are going to pass on your submission.

I really like your piece, so don't get me wrong. This all comes down to space, and we are flooded with so many submissions, the competition is fierce. Your article is really funny, but it's just not what we're looking for right now.

Please do not be discouraged. There are reasons your piece wasn't selected to be published versus others.

As the publisher and creator of the biggest satire/humor magazine on this platform, it's my duty to make sure the quality of each article meets strict standards of excellence. Your piece is solid, but it isn't as strong as the ten articles that I, my editors, and friends of ours wrote this past week. While it came close to being as good as one or two of them, it just wasn't quite as funny.

If it was, we would have published it.

Understand that we get hundreds of submissions each month, and we are only able to publish a few select pieces. For example, in August, I had to publish four of my own articles, so you can see how quickly things fill up. Add to that all the articles that our editors and friends of ours had published, and you can see just how tight things are over here.

I understand that some folks may see this as bias, considering the amount of material that appears in our publication that is written by either me, folks that work here, or our close friends, but I can assure you it isn't bias. Everyone here, including myself, has been featured in well-known publications and written some absolutely funny pieces, so, using that logic, if we have written some classically funny pieces, then it stands to reason that everything else would be just as good and most likely better than yours.

If it wasn't, it wouldn't get published in our magazine. You see what I'm saying?

Also, our process is thorough and hard on everyone, no matter who they are. For example, I wrote six pieces for our June edition earlier this year, and only five made it in. You see, just because I make the final decisions doesn't mean I won't reject articles from our staff, our friends, and even myself.

However, I get that this may not be enough to sway the doubts that we show favoritism. Consider this: you don't become the success we've become without serious credentials and a massive amount of talent. The people have spoken when you get to that level. It's a fact that if you're the biggest thing online, you must produce the best product. Look at the Kardashians, for example. Do you think they have achieved their level of success without serious credentials and talent to get them there?

Point is this: you don't get to where we are unless you're publishing the best possible pieces of satire. It just happens that it's mostly my work… or my friends and colleagues. What I mean is this: if what we published wasn't the best work, we wouldn't publish it. Trust me… it's that good, so that's why my stuff got in and yours didn't.

Bottom line: your piece is good, just not as good as the five of mine I'm publishing this week. If yours was as good, then we would publish it. It makes sense, right? I wouldn't publish five of mine if yours was just as good… instead, I would just publish four of mine next to yours.

Have you tried those other humor publications? There are even ones dedicated to publishing the ones we rejected. Although, just be prepared… the articles in those magazines are not as good as the stuff myself, our staff, and our friends write. I've had almost all of my pieces published in this magazine. Those folks haven't even had one. Yes, I may make the final decision on this, but if my stuff wasn't better, I wouldn't have published my pieces over theirs.

In conclusion, please feel free to continue submitting and don't give up just because of a rejection. You have a lot of talent, and with a little perseverance, I'm sure you'll eventually land in our publication… but probably not for a while. I just finished ten new articles, and they're all really, really funny.

# Think Globally and Act Locally in the Fight Against Climate Change: Get A Pool

Global warming is one of the most pressing challenges facing humanity today. Dare I say the most pressing? While some may balk at the idea that humans are radically altering the Earth in ways that will ultimately destroy the planet and humanity, the fact is, we are getting hotter. Be it a normal part of the Earth's cycle, as some may say, or the negative impact humans have had on the planet through industrialization, you cannot deny that you feel it every year.

It's fucking hot.

For those on the side that believe this is a very real threat and we Earthlings are the cause of it, they have a lot of science to back them and can point to how this is affecting our planet in tangible ways. As global temperatures rise, we can see the consequences become increasingly evident, specifically how it affects ecosystems and weather patterns. According to NASA and the National Oceanic and Atmospheric Administration, the Earth's average surface temperature has increased by approximately 2.12 degrees Fahrenheit since the late 19th century, with most of the warming occurring in the past forty years. The ten warmest years in the 143-year history of keeping records have all occurred since 2005, with the last nine years being the warmest.

This is a stark reality for Generation X'ers like me. Growing up, no one took the warnings on their can of hairspray seriously… that its contents were eating through the ozone layer. Aqua Net destroying the Earth? Get the fuck outta here!

However, it seems we were all wrong. I didn't believe it for a long time, but it's becoming clearer every year, with more and more evidence and scientific consensus, that there is a problem… and that problem cannot be denied. Increased atmospheric CO2 levels, melting polar ice and glaciers, increased frequency and intensity of extreme weather events, ocean acidification, and much more. These facts cannot be dismissed, and it took me a long time to really see it.

Now, I had been presented with all of this evidence for many years and blew most of it off. It wasn't until I did my own research that I became fully convinced that climate change is very real.

I went outside.

It's hotter than Paul Walker's last Sunday drive.

I had to do something. While the enormity of the issue can seem daunting, it is crucial to remember that every individual action contributes to the larger fight against the problem. I know this now. Each of us can play a significant role, emphasizing the collective power of personal responsibility. The Earth is getting hotter, so we need to do something about it.

However, I know what you're thinking: I'm just one person. What can I really do about global warming? I decided to go with the old motto "Think globally, act locally," so I got involved using that mindset as the driving factor, understanding that I can make adjustments in my life that actually affect change. I told my girlfriend… I said… "We can't actually go out there and take millions of gas-powered cars off the road or shut down industrial plants that are spewing tons of shit into the atmosphere, but we can make changes in our own home that will make a big difference."

At first, I thought she wouldn't back me. She's not a climate denier at all, but these would be changes that would alter how we live and drastically transform our existence. It also wasn't going to be cheap. Fighting global warming was going to be an investment. Luckily, she was 100 percent behind me.

The decision was made. We sold our house and bought one with an awesome pool in the backyard.

California has experienced record-breaking heat this summer. For nearly two weeks, across the western United States, temperatures were not only breaking records, but they were sustaining themselves for days into weeks. Where I live, we had record-breaking temperatures over 110 degrees for nearly 14 days straight, with one day hitting 118 degrees. This is all you need to experience to fully understand the impact that climate change is having on us.

But you know what? I didn't even notice it at all. I was in the pool every day… all day.

This life-changing decision to confront climate change head-on has made all the difference… and others need to get behind the movement to combat the problem because we're all dealing with it. I've met so many people who are worried about global warming, and I just tell them: "Hey, you just need to get a pool."

Sometimes I get a bit of backlash from climate deniers, despite scientific consensus strongly supporting the reality of global warming and its anthropogenic causes. There are some arguments made by skeptics. These arguments are generally less supported by the scientific community, but there are some legitimate points raised by those who argue against global warming.

The first is always the argument of natural climate variability. Skeptics argue that climate change is a natural process and that the Earth's climate has always fluctuated over geological timescales. Climate deniers often cite historical periods such as the Medieval Warm Period and the Little Ice Age as evidence that current warming trends could be part of a natural cycle. Before I was really shown the light of reality… before that day I walked out the door and said to myself: "God damn, it's so fucking hot the hydrants are fighting over the dogs."

I often defaulted to this argument as well. It's the go-to for almost every climate change denier.

Then we have to deal with the weaker arguments, such as questioning the accuracy of climate models. Critics claim that climate models, which predict future warming based on various greenhouse gas emission scenarios, are unreliable and overestimate the effects of CO2 on global temperatures. They argue that models are based on an incomplete understanding of climate systems and often fail to accurately predict short-term climate phenomena.

What the fuck does that even really mean? Have you been outside?

It's fucking hotter than Rick James' crack pipe on payday.

Even right now, with the hottest decade ever on record being the last ten years, climate deniers still try to twist the reality. They call it short-term temperature trends. They'll point to periods of temporary cooling or stabilization in global temperatures, such as the so-called "pause" or "hiatus" in warming observed in the early 21st century. They spin this bullshit and claim that these short-term trends indicate that long-term warming predictions are exaggerated. They'll even throw in solar activity just to sweeten the pot. Again, it's a bunch of mumbo-jumbo where they suggest that changes in solar radiation, not human activities, are the primary drivers of climate change.

Solar activity? Are you now trying to sell me panels to put on the roof of my house? Have you actually been outside?

It's fucking hotter than an asshole after a habanero-eating contest.

None of this has deterred me from fighting the fight against what we all know is happening to this planet. I can't change the world, but I can do small things to make a real difference. Get a pool. That was just the first move. I even bought a slushy machine and built a bar in the backyard to cool things down even more. Hell, I even installed misters along my gazebo because I feel like I have to do more than others are willing to do. That doesn't mean your contribution isn't valid, but I'm here for a larger purpose and when I put my heart into solving a problem that an individual can't possibly solve for the entire world, I'm going to go as far as I can as one man… I hope everyone else does too. If all you can do is buy a house with a pool, you're doing as much as anyone could expect. I applaud you. This isn't about what I do versus what you do. It's what we all can do together to make a difference. Again, think globally, act locally. Together we can beat this.

At the end of the day, this whole experience has been life-changing, and I've been humbled by doing my part to tackle a problem that is so much bigger than me. Don't call me any kind of hero. Hey… I'm just here to do my part.

# Kick a Gambling Habit by Betting $10,000 That You Can Do It

Never bet more than you can afford to lose.

This popular saying is probably the most common phrase most everyone hears at one time or another in their life and has become the base starting point for everyone who decides to gamble. For most Americans, gambling is a casual form of entertainment, usually part of a trip to one of many cities where it is legalized, Las Vegas being the premier destination. This is usually a secondary part of some larger event, be it a bachelor party or holiday trip like New Year's Eve. Most people who visit gambling destinations gamble as a peripheral activity… that's most people, but not all.

For many folks, gambling is an addiction, and it affects millions of people. For me specifically, I was never enamored enough with gambling to see the attraction. Also, I'm cheap as fuck. I eat cereal with a fork so I can save the milk for a second helping, so you won't see me dropping too much money on a table in hopes that a marble lands on red or black.

Regardless of my situation, gambling addiction is very real. It can lead to financial ruin, the destruction of relationships, and can be attached to mental health problems, as the spiral of the addiction can lead addicts to live in a perpetual cycle of trying to get back what they have lost. Helping solve the problem needs a systematic approach. It is a tiered system where we first need to start at the very top, then work our way down the tiers.

The first thing you need to do is find a bookie who is willing to take a $10,000 bet that you can stop gambling.

Big money on the line will be the anchor for successfully overcoming your addiction. When you have a lot to lose, you'll be much more motivated and, if you're successful, you'll have a lot to win. Also, consider finding someone who will, at minimum, physically hurt you, or worse, slaughter your whole family, if you fail to come through with your end of the bet. The fear of being permanently injured or having your family wiped out is a great motivator.

Betting on yourself that you can quit gambling is also the first step in admitting you have a problem. The journey to recovery has to start here. Denial is a common barrier. For example, your claim that gambling has brought your family closer together because you lost your house and had to move into a small apartment is clearly denial. For individuals struggling with gambling addiction, putting up $10,000 is accepting the reality of the situation and acknowledging the need for change.

After we have the motivator, we move to the next tiers that provide us the actual steps to stop gambling. Before we can do this, we need to understand exactly what gambling addiction is. Gambling addiction is primarily characterized by uncontrollable urges to gamble despite the outcome of a given gambling run. For most normal folks, losing too much money makes them rethink whether they want to continue gambling, ultimately leaving them less rich than when they started but still left with most of the money they showed up with. For addicts, they'll likely be in the bathroom at Circus Circus giving a blowjob to some random drunk frat guy because they're 100 percent sure the New York Giants are going to cover the spread and need $50 to get in on the action. It's a lock, so having a stranger rest his nuts on your chin is worth it. We can't lose. This addiction can be driven by various factors, including psychological, genetic, and environmental influences, but often can be driven by having no shame and no problem blowing complete strangers when you have nothing left to hock at the pawn shop. Understanding the root cause of the addiction is the first step toward recovery.

After we place a $10,000 bet that you can do it, we move into the next tier. That is to get professional help, but that requires us to know where to go. Most people understand there are many services for all kinds of addictions but may be unaware there are similar services for compulsive gambling. The most well-known is 1–800-GAMBLER. This is a great place to start for help with a gambling problem. Now, I have to make this clear for those who are addicted to gambling. This is a helpline for a gambling problem, meaning the problem of addiction. This isn't a helpline for situations when you're at the blackjack table showing an ace and a three, with the dealer showing a six, wanting to know if you should hit or not. That's not the type of gambling problem they specialize in.

The next tier is to develop a strong support network. This is vital. Your network can include family, friends, support groups, and professionals. However, it's important to also make sure that the folks around you are in the same mindset. For example, you want people who recognize that getting back on your feet means stopping gambling, not gambling to the point where you lose your car and now have to walk everywhere. That's not the meaning of "getting back on your feet" we're talking about. We need clear and open communication with support members that can foster understanding, but we have to accept that not everyone will be there for you or provide that support. If they decide to leave you because of your gambling addiction, betting them that they won't will likely not work. You might think they're bluffing, but I don't think reading people is your strength. Look at your gambling record. Most of your calls have been coin flips, and half the time it's a two-headed coin with you calling tails.

The next tier is to replace gambling with healthy habits. This is a crucial part of the recovery process. Now, some will turn to exercise or develop new hobbies, which is great and can help, but hobbies and going to the gym can only consume so much of your time. With that in mind, some will opt to move toward religion and start to spend more time at the church helping others, which is not a bad idea for two specific reasons. The first reason is that many programs attached to recovery from addictions do have a religious component, so it will complement the time you spend in church. The second reason is this can take up a lot of your time and keep you occupied more so than hobbies or exercise, for example. Even if you're not particularly religious or totally buy into church, this is fine. Think of it as a support network and an opportunity to help others. Even if you're a total atheist, you should consider getting involved. Every atheist who is a recovering gambling addict has some connection to God. While you may see people in church praying, thinking that it's all bullshit, just remember that you were once at a blackjack table praying that the dealer draws any card six or higher. You may look at that guy in church praying and question whether he means it, but you know damn well when you were in the casino, you fucking meant it. Don't question their faith. That dealer drawing a king prevented you from having to bend over a railing behind the Tropicana to get back on the table. You think you feel a "hot streak" about to pop, but I can assure you that the hot streak you would have felt behind the Tropicana would have nothing to do with gambling.

Finally, we all understand that kicking a gambling habit is challenging but, at the end of the day, an achievable goal. It requires a multifaceted approach. Now, we have $10,000 on the line, a clear plan, and all the tools for success at our disposal. Just remember, if you can stop gambling, you will come away with the four-to-one odds the bookie gave you, and that $40,000 will be a nice start to a new life. After you collect, you can tell your wife to pack her bags because you just won $40,000. When she asks if she should pack for a vacation trip to somewhere warm or for a destination that is colder, just tell her that you don't give a fuck what she packs, as long as she is out of the house by noon.

With the right strategies and support, individuals can break free from the grip of gambling addiction and lead a healthier, more fulfilling life… one that doesn't include that bitch who will give you zero credit nor ever recognize what you just accomplished, still finding some other dumbass shit to nag you about.

# My Grief Counselor Was So Good, When He Died, I Didn't Care

In August of 2020, I lost my mother suddenly to a heart attack. A few months later, my father passed from a long illness. The deaths of my parents were one of the hardest, if not the hardest, things I've ever had to deal with.

I'm still dealing with it today.

However, things have gotten so much better, and I can thank one person for this: Dr. Tiberious G. Fontana, or Dr. T for short. If he is not the greatest grief counselor in the United States, I would guarantee he is the best in California.

This man saved my life. I mean that literally. I was on the verge of doing something very drastic and felt completely hopeless after the loss of my parents. He brought me back to a place where I could not only deal with the grief of my parents' passing, but also find my purpose for getting out of bed every day. I love this man more than anyone I have ever met, and I do not say that lightly. He may be the only person who could have saved me.

This man not only taught me the skills to deal with my grief but also guided me through a whole new way of thinking about my family and myself, in ways that have opened up lanes of consciousness I never knew existed. He has made handling grief no longer an issue for me.

Dr. T is so good at what he does that when he died, I didn't care… I didn't give any fucks that he was dead.

Again, this is a man that I loved and a man that saved my life. When he had a massive heart attack, I didn't even feel one ounce of grief. That's how amazing he is… or was.

And it's not that I felt nothing after he died. It's a bummer, for sure, and I grieved for an appropriate amount of time… or something like that… you know what I mean.

Dr. T and I were out having dinner at the Royal Oaks Steakhouse, which we did once a month as part of "checking in" and seeing how I was doing. It really wasn't a typical session because he had taught me so much about handling grief that I wasn't in that state of mind anymore.

On this particular evening we were joined by other patients of Dr. T, all of whom had been just as successful as myself in dealing with their grief. We were all having a good time when Dr. T began to complain about shortness of breath. Then suddenly, he just fell to the ground.

The waitress came running over and screamed, "Does anyone know CPR!?"

I was sipping on my martini and said, "I know the entire alphabet."

Everyone at our table laughed. Well, except for one person.

The waitress was clearly upset.

"You think someone dying is funny?"

"Darling, life doesn't cease to be funny when someone dies any more than it ceases to be serious when someone laughs."

Dr. T taught me that, by the way.

Look, grief is a weird animal, and we all have to deal with it in healthy ways, even if the ways some people deal with it seem odd or even unhealthy to the untrained eye.

For example, Albert, one of the guys at the table with us that night, lost his best friend Tommy in a horrible accident years ago. Tommy was his childhood friend who had been there his whole life and was the best man at his wedding. His death was brutal on Albert. Dr. T told him to find a way to honor his friend's memory and to keep his memory alive. At the time of Tommy's death, Albert's wife was eight months pregnant, and he decided to name the child after his best friend. However, this didn't adequately help Albert with his grief. Dr. T told him to teach his newborn all about Tommy and allow his child to become a kind of walking encyclopedia for him, ensuring that his memory lives on. Albert took this one step further and began to pray to God that his newborn child would actually be reincarnated into his old friend. Dr. T didn't like this idea and thought it was unhealthy, but allowed Albert to buy into the possibility that his son could be reincarnated as Tommy. When Albert's son turned ten, he looked nearly identical to his best friend. It was uncanny how much his son looked like Tommy. Maybe it was a miracle. I mean, how else could you explain that? Whatever it was, it was the key for Albert to make peace with Tommy's passing. He has never been in a better space.

That's the one thing about Dr. T that made him special… he was open to whatever could possibly help people not only deal with their grief but move past it, even if it seemed unorthodox.

This is probably best highlighted in my life when my friend Gabe died in a drowning accident. I was slated to give the eulogy but was very stricken with grief and wasn't sure how to best handle the situation. Much like Albert, Dr. T taught me how to step into the person's existence and honor who they were when they were alive. What would Gabe want you to do? Dr. T gave me the tools I needed to not only cope with Gabe's death but understand what Gabe needed from me, which allowed me to move past the grief.

In the middle of my eulogy, I pulled out a life jacket, walked over to the casket, and laid it on top of him. Everyone was confused, many of them seemingly upset that I would do this. His mother yelled at me.

"What are you doing!? What is that!?"

"It's a life jacket," I said in a matter-of-fact tone.

"Why would you put a life jacket in the casket of someone who drowned!?"

"What the fuck is wrong with you?!" someone else yelled from the back of the crowd.

"Well, it's what he would have wanted," I replied to everyone.

The whole funeral seemed really upset with this. I tried to explain how Dr. T taught me that fully understanding what Gabe would want would help me cope with his death. They didn't get it and threw me out of the funeral. At first, I was devastated that I was tossed from my friend's funeral, but Dr. T did such amazing work over the years that after about five minutes, I didn't give a shit. That is the gift that Dr. T gave to the world: the ability to handle the inevitable grief we all will face, and in some cases, the type of grief that could eventually devastate one's life if not properly dealt with.

The man was a saint and I miss him a lot… well, kind of… whatever.

# How are My Chalk Outlines of Dead Folks Not Considered Art?

If you're murdered or die in some other mysterious way, you may have me as the artist that draws up your chalk outline. If so, God forbid, that's you laying in the street, then it's me on the scene: the artist. Yes, it is art, and people need to recognize that.

Let's just say you had an unfortunate brush with death.

It's baffling to me that I have laid down some of the dopest chalk outlines ever seen, yet chumps like Banksy and Shepard Fairey get all the accolades. Their street art just exists in the street. My shit is actually on the fuckin' street… unless the dude was mowed down in a drive-by shooting while standing on the side of Lucky's Liquor Store. Then it becomes a 90-degree-angled piece that includes both the street and the wall.

Who the fuck has ever done dope-ass pieces like this? No one. Yet still no recognition. On top of that, those guys can create art anytime they want. My art is much more special and rare because I have to wait until some motherfucker is killed.

One time I went to a homicide scene where the dude was sitting up in his bed when his wife took a 12-gauge to his face. I busted out my best set of chalk to draw him from his bedsheets, up a headboard, then onto the wall where his chinbone lodged into the sheetrock. That outline was fucking legendary, covering three different canvases of fabric, wood, and drywall. Plus, I decorated around that outline with contour lines, basically creating an emphasis on the person's boundaries and significant internal lines.

That's right, I don't just outline bodies. I make the perfection of form and beauty that is contained in the sum of all men… even if some of the man is splattered across the wall.

I'm chalk full of creativity, bitches.

The problem with folks is they see a dead body and say, "Why?" I see a dead body and say, "Why not?" Life is art and art is life… even if it involves a bunch of corpses. I don't separate the two, even if the person I'm working with is separated in two from a horrible industrial machine accident.

This is the way it's always been. You see, as a kid, my dream was to be an artist. My teachers laughed at my crayon drawings, especially Mr. Sanderson, who mocked my art relentlessly, until he became one of my finest pieces of work. I chalked his mangled body after he hit a tree and flew out his front window. No disrespect either. I don't care what he said to me as a kid. I immortalized his stiff corpse on the corner of 42nd and Wilson Street, where the moonlit sky and stars danced in harmony with the wind, and the spirit of the haunting calm was only awakened from its slumber by a drunk that slammed into a tree at 75 miles per hour.

That piece caught every essence of the night as the lady of death became my muse once again. This time, though, something was viscerally different. From the shattered windshield to the curb where his bottle of Old Crow landed to his jacket that was hanging from the tree, my approach had to be restructured in what I did in terms of... of... well... um... To be honest, I'm not sure what I'm saying here. Look, if I could say it in words, there would be no reason to chalk the art in the first place, right?

Maybe if you all chalked a mile in my shoes, you'd get it.

Then there was the guy that jumped off the twenty-third floor of the Mid-Town Falkland Towers. His body was so contorted and twisted that I had to channel my inner Daniel Browning Smith to get the outline done. When I finished, folks were comparing it to *The Scream* by Edvard Munch. It was pure proto-expressionism at its highest level. It's another reminder that even though I had to become a fucking contortionist myself to pull this piece off, I'm not paid for my labor, but rather for my vision.

This should have been the piece that broke me into mainstream success, but as soon as the investigation was over, the neighborhood kids divided the piece up into sections and turned it into hopscotch.

Whatever.

Bottom line is this: The art community values authenticity and genuine passion for the craft. That's the way it's always been. If you genuinely love what you do and are proud of your work, there's nothing wrong with expressing pride in what you lay down. However, it's important to do so in a way that invites others into the conversation rather than pushing them away, which is why I still don't understand my lack of legitimacy and mainstream success. I'm all-inclusive, baby! If your punk-ass gets stabbed fifty times tonight, I'm there drawing up a masterpiece until daylight.

I don't care who you are... I turn the murder scene into a one-man gallery that would rival Art Basel's Art Unlimited Exhibition.

Maybe the problem is communication. Maybe I don't communicate well enough how my art matters. Instead of outright bragging, I should consider framing my accomplishments as a story or a journey. Share the creative process, challenges, and growth, which can be more engaging and relatable.

I can walk you through that one time a diesel truck hit a VW Bug and how I had to use the Jaws of Life just to get to the body. The whole process was reminiscent of allover painting. This is an abstract expressionist approach where the entire composition is given equal attention... and let me tell you, the man that was in that VW was all over the place, so every inch of that car was given equal attention. I came at this piece with the entire area covered in chalk, brushstrokes, finger blending, and a bunch of color techniques as I worked with unorthodox materials embedded into the surface, such as the guy's AM radio javelined through his skull and the camshaft mashed through his lower body.

I don't know. Maybe one day I will be recognized, but if by some slim chance that never happens, it's okay. The reality is this: An artist cannot fail... it is a success just to be one. The truth is I'm likely to follow the path of so many other great artists throughout history. I'll die, and then suddenly my work will be recognized. I just hope whoever chalk outlines my body puts some respect on that piece. Just remember who paved the way for you and the rest of these artists to have the opportunity to chase such greatness.

# The Solution to America's Homeless Crisis: Move to a Better Part of Town

The homelessness crisis remains one of the most pressing and complex issues of our time, affecting millions of individuals and families across the nation. Rooted in economic inequality, lack of affordable housing, mental health challenges, drug addiction, and systemic failures, homelessness is one of the most multifaceted and difficult issues facing America today... and it only seems to be getting worse the more the country tries to address the problem. There is no doubt. There are a ton of homeless everywhere, the numbers are growing, and some fatalists are now claiming there is no solution to the problem.

Well, they're wrong... and I have the answer.

Despite the fact that everything from government programs to tough love have all failed, the answer to this seemingly unsolvable puzzle is quite simple. So simple, in fact, it's been overlooked by every expert in the field of social sciences.

You don't want anyone on the streets? Then move to a part of town where there isn't anyone on the streets.

First, I don't want to take credit for this solution, because I certainly didn't come up with this answer during some powerful meeting of the minds with the world's intellectual elite. I discovered this solution on accident. I spent my entire life living in areas where homelessness was a constant issue, be it a minor scattering of individuals to large camps close to where I lived. I have always lived near homeless folks. However, after years of struggling to land a high-paying job, I finally secured one that quadrupled my salary, and that enabled me to move to the wealthy side of town.

For the last six months, I haven't seen a single homeless person. At one point, I had gone so long without seeing any homeless that I forgot they existed. I realized I hadn't even thought about the issue in months. Looks like the problem has been solved, even if my friends tell me it hasn't been solved. They say I'm just willfully ignorant, living in the fantasy world of "out of sight, out of mind." To-MAY-to, ta-MA-to. Aren't we just splitting hairs here? Now, I do not want to come across as some cold son-of-a-bitch that doesn't care about homeless folks, because my track record says otherwise.

I used to regularly give $1 to every homeless man I ran into. Same with any homeless women… well, not exactly. I would only give the women .77 cents. Look, my point is this: Despite my proposed solution of moving the fuck out of those neighborhoods, I have nothing but the deepest sympathy for those struggling to find housing and have always helped out with a few spare dollars when I could. This isn't about ignoring or running away from the problem. If anything, I have always hit the problem head-on and defended the homeless from uncaring assholes that criticized me, claiming I was perpetuating the problem by giving handouts.

One time I was walking home from the liquor store, and a homeless guy stopped me and asked for $5, which I was more than happy to give to him. The old lady walking behind me stopped and said, "You know he is only going to use that $5 for drugs." I was stunned… really? I turned to her just to clarify her comment.

"You're telling me that he is going to use this $5 to buy drugs?"

She nodded yes.

I looked back at the homeless man and confronted him about this. I needed to know exactly where I could also get drugs for $5.

And this isn't a unique situation for me. I run into these situations all the time.

When I first got the apartment in my old neighborhood, a homeless guy asked me for money, but all I had on me were $100 bills. That's a lot of money. I was conflicted with what to do. Do I really want a $100 to go toward alcohol, drugs, and probably some really unsanitary sexual favor later that night? No, I didn't want that at all… so I gave him the money. This was a major moment of growth for me. Up to this point, I never paid any mind to them, like they weren't real people. That day I learned these are folks with histories and families. Prior to this, I never gave the homeless money for two reasons: One, they want to buy drugs and alcohol with that money, and two, I wanted to buy drugs and alcohol with that money.

Regardless of how my attitude changed over the years, the situation has always been this way since I can remember. I always had homeless folks around me. It was an integral part of my life's fabric. I was taught the homeless problem stemmed from social conditions, drugs, mental illness, and other systemic factors, which all made sense until I recently moved. Now I realize it really isn't that complicated. The problem really doesn't stem from all these economic and social factors as much as it stems from the fact that I was poor as fuck and had to live in the ghetto with all these unhoused motherfuckers.

And these numbers are staggering.

According to the U.S. Department of Housing and Urban Development (HUD), as of the most recent data, over 580,000 people experience homelessness on any given night. This figure includes individuals sleeping in shelters, transitional housing, and those unsheltered on the streets. One of the most concerning trends is the growing number of unsheltered homelessness, where individuals lack access to temporary shelters and live in cars, abandoned buildings, or public spaces. Approximately 40% of those experiencing homelessness are unsheltered, highlighting a severe lack of affordable housing options and support systems.

Families and youth are particularly vulnerable, with nearly 30% of the homeless population consisting of families with children. Additionally, over 10% are unaccompanied youth under the age of

25, a group disproportionately affected by foster care instability, abuse, and financial hardship.

Homelessness also disproportionately affects marginalized groups. Black Americans, who make up about 13% of the U.S. population, account for 39% of the homeless population. Similarly, Native Americans and Hispanic individuals experience higher rates of homelessness compared to white Americans.

Now, in my state of California, things are really bad, despite Governor Gavin Newsom having done a number of things to help solve the problem. He emphasized increasing housing production by cutting red tape, streamlining approvals, and investing over $40 billion in housing initiatives. His administration set a legally binding goal of planning 2.5 million homes within six years and launched the Housing Accountability Unit to enforce housing laws. In 2024, Newsom ordered the clearing of homeless encampments, encouraging local governments to use state funds for housing and intervention programs. He also signed a package of 32 housing bills aimed at enforcing state housing laws more strictly and penalizing cities that resist new housing and homeless shelter construction.

Despite these efforts, California continues to face challenges in reducing homelessness, with the state's homeless population remaining significant... in other words, nothing he has done has improved shit. All that time, money, resources, and years of implementation that included thousands of people and tens of thousands of man-hours has changed nothing.

My solution can take as little as a zero percent down payment and a 30-day escrow. Boom! Problem solved.

Again, I know what you're thinking. The problem has not been solved, and just because I don't see any of it doesn't mean it isn't there. This isn't really accurate. It depends on how you look at it. I would counter with this: When you clean your house each week, do you pull out your refrigerator or stove to clean behind them every time? Probably not. Why? Because we know if you can't see it, it must not be dirty. After you spend a day cleaning your house spotless but don't clean behind the refrigerator and stove, are you going to say your house is dirty? No... it's fucking clean. You wouldn't say otherwise.

At the end of the day, maybe you think I'm insensitive. Some would point out that just because I have a great job and a new house on the rich side of town doesn't mean I couldn't end up in the same situation. According to research from Charles Schwab, 59% of Americans are considered to be one paycheck away from homelessness. This is true. I have seen things like this happen.

I met a homeless man once that shared his story of how he ended up homeless, and it was this exact story. He told me that up until the prior week, he had it all. He had a roof over his head, plenty to eat with all the food being cooked by others, his clothes were washed and pressed by a staff of folks, he had a gym that was mere feet away from his bedroom, a library, and an outdoor recreation area that had its own basketball court. He said bills were not an issue, he had no debt, and had full medical coverage. All of this was gone in the span of a few days.

I felt sorry for him. I asked, "What happened? Drugs? Alcohol? Divorce?"

"Oh no, nothing like that," he said. "I was finally released from prison."

So, I get it. No one is immune from the reality that no matter how good you have it, homelessness can hit you fast regardless of your circumstances.

At the end of the day, most would say that simply moving away from it doesn't change anything, but I would wholeheartedly disagree. It *does* solve the homeless issue… for me. You can call me anti-homeless, or homelessist… if there is an "ist" for homeless folks. Maybe it's called nohomophobic. Either way, you would be wrong. I'm still here to support the unhoused anytime I can. For example, just the other day I was back in my old neighborhood and I gave a homeless man $500 and an iPhone. You wouldn't believe how much joy that gave me, especially when he put the gun away.

# Not Everyone Can Be A Doctor. The World Needs Garbage Men Too… I Did Both

For the teachers that constantly dropped the cliché that not everyone can be a doctor, that the world needs garbage men too, let me rest these nuts on your chin.

I did both, you bitches.

Damn straight. In December, I received my PhD in Animal Husbandry and Assessment from Morehead State University, and I've just completed my first six months on the job as a sanitation engineer, aka, a garbage man, for the sanitation district in Booger Hole, West Virginia.

Yeah, Booger Hole is a real place.

In hindsight, Morehead State University probably wasn't the best choice, considering I had offers from schools with way better reputations. I was suckered into thinking it would be a total party college. It's called Morehead… who doesn't want that? They should put a disclaimer on their website. That PhD program was no joke. I busted my ass, and they grinded my soul down to the nubs. I got more anxiety, debt, and an ulcer, but didn't get any more head. Nonetheless, it doesn't matter at this point. I got the degree and the job, and that's all that really counts.

Being a garbage man with a PhD puts me in a unique position. No one at work can tell me anything. I have more education than everyone, even my boss. He only has a bachelor's degree.

Pathetic.

Even communicating with him is like talking to a child. I showed up to work after taking the day off, and he tells me I need to go get tested and cleared of the coronavirus before I could return. What? I said I'm not coming in because I have a case of Corona. I didn't say I came down with a case of coronavirus.

Dumbass. You see what I mean?

Same with my coworkers. They're even worse.

I was riding with this guy Jerry, who never stopped talking about politics, philosophy, and offering his moronic opinions about how we can do our work more efficiently. He complained that the boss never listened to him. No shit. You barely graduated high school and dropped out of community college. What earth-shattering ideas could you possibly have?

Jerry would get combative, saying that a PhD doesn't make me any smarter than anyone else. He actually said it made me even more myopic and closed-minded. Note here… he didn't use those specific words. You think an idiot like him would even know those words?

"Sean, you need to think outside of the box."

He said that to me constantly.

At a sanitation convention in Las Vegas, Jerry and I got into an argument about the glass windows in our hotel. He told me they were shatterproof to prevent anyone from breaking the glass and jumping to their death. I told him there is no such thing as shatterproof glass, that all glass can be shattered to some degree. I learned that in college.

He wouldn't let it go, so just to prove me wrong, he ran as fast as he could and jumped into the window. It didn't shatter, but it popped out of the frame and he fell 30 floors to his death. The glass hit the ground next to him and shattered.

You see, Jerry, I was right.

At his funeral, I walked up to his casket and asked him: "Who's thinking outside of the box now?"

The residents I serve aren't much smarter either, that's for sure.

One morning I pulled up to a house where a guy was talking to some cops in his driveway. When I attempted to pick up the garbage, the cop stopped me and told me to wait a minute. I guess the truck's noise was making it hard to talk to the resident. It seems the guy's wife disappeared the week before and hadn't been located. Not a trace of her anywhere.

The cop tells him, in his experience, that if they don't find someone after the first 48 hours, he can expect the worst. Suddenly, the man starts yelling at me to hold up and wait while he pulled all of his wife's possessions out of the trash cans.

What the fuck? I'm on a schedule, dude.

This is the kind of shit I have to put up with, but it's worth it. The job sucks, but who cares. I showed them all. I got my PhD and became a garbage man. I'm gonna take a picture with my PhD, wearing those classic Bulwark midweight classic coveralls with reflective trim, and send it to all my high school teachers.

Kiss my ass, y'all! I'm a doctor and a garbage man. When I return for my high school reunion, I better see this picture hanging in the front office or a banner with my accomplishments hanging from the ceiling of the gymnasium.

# There Are Three Doors In Hell... And I Got To Pick One

Is there life after death?

We've all seen them... folks who say they have crossed over to the other side after dying for a short period of time. I'm sure you know exactly what I'm talking about: the near-death experience. I never had much of an opinion about the validity of these claims. I always felt it was possible, but at the same time, I had my doubts. This would all change last year.

I had my own near-death experience after a horrific car accident that left me dead for nearly three minutes. After I was revived, I told everyone what happened to me and what happens to you after you die. I was there. I lived it... sort of... I mean, I was *dead.* You know what I mean.

However, the accounts of my near-death experience were mostly met with scoffs and doubters who thought I was exaggerating what had happened, at best. Some openly said it never happened. My girlfriend, in particular, said that driving a go-kart into the wall at an amusement park while drunk is not a "horrific car accident," but I fail to see the difference. The fact is, I still died in a car accident... or maybe just knocked myself into a brief coma... or maybe I was just unconscious... or just passed out from excessive drinking. Whatever, bruh, you weren't there.

Let's not debate semantics. To-MAY-to. To-MAA-to. Based on all the medical evidence I was able to gather from Google, WebMD, and that doctor at the farmacia I talked with in Mexico, I was dead. Let me tell you this: Hell is real. I went there. I know exactly what it's like. This may shock many of you. Hell does have three doors to choose from, and I had to choose one.

I also learned that God and Satan often have conversations with each other and both organizations, Heaven and Hell, operate like any other organization on Earth. There are procedures, protocols, and employees who run them… and it isn't a perfect system. Like any other organization, they make mistakes.

When I tell folks this, it's the first thing they criticize and the main thing they lean on to discredit me. They say that's impossible. "God doesn't make mistakes."

Wrong.

Aren't we, as humans, made in God's image? We make mistakes constantly. Hell, if I just accidentally mixed up two letters while writing this, the whole essay could be urined.

During my journey to Hell, an engineer who died from cancer showed up. He was absolutely livid because he was a devout Christian, yet he was in Hell. He wanted answers. He tried to explain this to a demon who was pushing some kind of afterlife paperwork, but there was a line a million miles long with a bunch of damned spirits. Eventually, St. Peter's office assistant, if that's what they would be called, phoned down to Hell and insisted there was a mistake. The engineer was supposed to be in Heaven.

"Double-check the paperwork," the voice echoed from the clouds above.

The demon didn't seem interested, insisting that he already checked the paperwork and told Heaven to double-check *their* paperwork.

After this went up the chain of command, with a few managers and other higher officials from both sides going back and forth, God finally showed up and demanded to talk with Satan to get this straightened out. Satan was adamant that his paperwork was accurate and that no mistakes were made by St. Peter. No pun intended, but there was no way in Hell he was going to return the engineer to Heaven.

This is where it got ugly. God threatened to sue Satan and the whole Hell organization from top to bottom.

Satan just laughed.

"Sue me? You're in Heaven, God… where are you going to find a lawyer?"

I get it. It doesn't match any description of Hell you've ever heard of, but that's what actually gives me credibility. You know why no one has ever described Hell like this? It's because very few have been there and come back to talk about it. I'm giving you a first-hand, real account of it, so it's not going to be like what you see on television or read about in books.

The engineer mix-up was not the only mistake. I heard a demon making fun of St. Peter, recounting the day Adolf Hitler died and showed up to the gates of Heaven to be judged. There wasn't any discussion or conferences to go over paperwork. It's Hitler. There is no discussion. Immediately, St. Peter shouted, "Hell, Hitler!" However, Jesus thought he said "Heil, Hitler" and let him into Heaven.

It took days to correct the paperwork and make sure Hitler was sent to his proper spot in Hell.

Regardless of all of this, I'm here to tell you that the old joke about going to Hell and having to choose a door out of three is a real thing. I experienced it. Why that is a common joke in the living world still baffles me... I assume it comes from an interpretation of some part of the Holy Bible, and over thousands of years, it got twisted and turned into a cliché for jokes. However, I have done extensive and intense research of the Holy Bible and have not come across any passage I can interpret as discussing anything about three doors to choose from. Well, to be honest, I have actually only done extensive research on Google and Reddit. No one is saying anything about three doors and the Holy Bible. Same thing, essentially.

Nonetheless, I was there. I was offered to pick one of three doors. We all know what this means... no matter what door you pick, you're fucked. It's Hell's version of a mind game to simply screw with you one last time before you spend eternity in damnation.

I wasn't going to play that game.

When offered the doors, I went into a fit hoping I could gain some leverage for negotiation.

"Oh, fuck! How original! Three doors to choose from, as if any of these doors make a difference!" I screamed. "Really? I come all the way to Hell and this is the shit you put in front of me? Fucking rookies! All of you! This is really embarrassing for you."

The demon that presented the three doors to me looked rattled. I had gotten inside his head. Still, he was steadfast in the "three-door method." I'm assuming his stubbornness was coming from his boss, Satan, so he had no choice but to stand his ground. However, the awkwardness was there. He was dealing with some humiliation. The more I ridiculed him, the more he got frustrated, until he cracked under the scrutiny.

"Alright," the demon said, "how about this. I'll let you look behind each door before you choose. Are you satisfied, big shot? How about that?"

I smiled, knowing that he was pulling shit out of his ass, desperate to recover from my initial berating. I knew it didn't matter, because all options would suck, but I took this as a small victory.

"Yeah, I'm in… what's behind door number one?"

He opened the door, and there were billions and billions of people standing on their heads on a concrete floor.

First thought was this: I do not want to spend eternity standing on top of my head on concrete. I don't have any clue what's behind door numbers two or three, but it wouldn't surprise me if it's ten times worse than what's behind door number one. All I could do at this point was pray… yeah, I'm in Hell praying. Maybe I should have prayed before arriving here. It's spilt milk at this point.

"Okay, what's behind door number two?"

He opened the second door, and there were billions and billions of people standing on their heads on a wooden floor. It's better than concrete, but still nothing nice. Spending an eternity standing on your head on a wooden floor is not a substantial upgrade. This was a good sign. The second door was better than the first door, so we're moving in the right direction.

"Yeah, I see where this is going, demon. What's behind the third door? Is it eternity on your head on carpet? Is that what's behind door number three?"

The demon smirked.

He opened the third door, and there were billions and billions of people standing knee-deep in chicken shit drinking coffee. Okay… this is different. Not ideal. I hate the smell of chicken shit, but I did like coffee when I was alive, so, in reality, this wasn't so bad compared to doors one or two.

The choice was obvious. I took door number three and walked through, sealing my fate... or so I thought. That's when everything changed, and I was called back to Earth. I returned to the world of the living. The EMT splashed a large cup of water in my face, and a bright light struck me across my eyes, returning me to the ordinary world.

However, from here on out, all I've gotten was shit from folks who not only don't believe what I experienced, but claim I never died in the first place... nor do they believe water can bring you back from the dead. On an unrelated note, I'm no longer invited to funerals because throwing water on the deceased is apparently "desecrating the body." Whatever... I'm not here to convince you because I know the truth.

Oh, by the way. Coffee break is over. Back on your head.

# Fakespeare: The Worst Writing Advice I Have Ever Heard

It didn't seem to matter whether it was a short story or a novel; there are some things I was told about writing that simply weren't all that helpful. Not because it was bad advice, but because it seemed more like common sense disguised as some key to unlocking the door to producing a great piece of writing.

It was like telling someone the secret to becoming rich is by learning this one little-known trick: make sound investments. Thanks, Warren Buffett.

Over the years, working as a journalist and as a writer of fiction, short stories, and novels, I was told a variety of things that were presented as answers to the mystery of unlocking the power of any written piece. "Do you write like a clueless high school freshman who failed 8th-grade English? Learn these secrets and you'll be drafting works that rival Hemingway and Steinbeck."

To make matters worse, it wasn't just that the advice was basically common sense, but a lot of it told you *what* to do without actually telling you *how* to do it. This is probably the biggest frustration with bad advice… it may not even be bad, and we all can benefit from it. However, those giving it rarely explain *how*.

Let's start with the worst piece of advice I ever received: "Make sure you create conflict." This is one of the strangest things to tell any writer because it's about as basic as it gets. Almost every story ever written has conflict. That's the heart. Conflict is so essential to storytelling that informing someone to "make sure you have conflict" is like telling an aspiring mechanic that a car needs an engine to run.

"Wait… let me get this straight… you're telling me without an engine, this car doesn't move?"

Exactly. Thanks for the invaluable information. At least this piece of advice doesn't really require you to explain *how* to do it. I get it… create some kind of conflict.

Competing for the worst advice I ever received, and another one that seems like common sense, is telling writers that they need to give the reader a hero… someone they can root for, get behind… or even hate. Basically, someone to care about. This is also about as basic an idea as it can get. The advice is almost never explained in any depth, which would be helpful.

Okay, I get it… characters that people care about. How do I do that?

Crickets.

Now, I know creating interesting characters is complicated and not easily explained, but most advice about this rarely gives even the framework for what makes a character have the desired depth or qualities that draw readers in. Can you at least drop a few nuggets of wisdom? Can you at least give me an example?

Appeal to the five senses in your writing is another piece of advice that baffles me. If anyone has done any significant reading in their life, they probably already know this. And if they don't, they likely do it on accident anyway when they write. Most folks will default initially to focusing on what characters "see," but how would anyone tell a story without including the other four senses, even if they consciously didn't think to do so? It's almost impossible to write a story, even a bad one, without including the other senses.

Another common piece of advice is about the power of dialogue: use dialogue to create memorable characters and bring a story to life. Dialogue is massively important, and this may be helpful for some newer writers. However, for even amateur writers, this isn't mind-blowing. I understood the concept even before I decided to write anything and quickly realized how crucial dialogue is in making a story truly spectacular.

Again… *how do I do that?* Give me an example, at least.

I could probably write a lot more about this, but at this point, if you're still reading, you're probably calling me all kinds of names and asking, "Well then, genius… what advice do you have since you're so smart?"

There are two things you need to create a great piece of writing: a really good story and captivating, dynamic characters working within that story. That's it. If you have these two things, you're likely going to knock it out of the park.

Now, I know what you're thinking: didn't I just do what I criticized others for doing? I just spouted out something most writers already know, and I certainly didn't explain how to actually do these two things.

Maybe it's because developing a good story and interesting characters is not something that can really be taught. Sure, I can probably give you examples of this greatness and some basic framework that I learned, but that doesn't mean you're suddenly going to be able to do it… and who ever said I was able to do it? I never claimed any expertise… I can't even spell expertise.

Welcome to the wonderful world of writing… and follow me on social media to connect with me, so I can give you more advice you don't want or need.

www.ingramcontent.com/pod-product-compliance
Lightning Source LLC
Chambersburg PA
CBHW060909140726
47996CB00001B/179